F

Suffering Mothers
in Mid-Victorian Novels

Suffering Mothers
in Mid-Victorian Novels

by Natalie J. McKnight

St. Martin's Press
New York

35249488
DLC

11-30-00

SUFFERING MOTHERS IN MID-VICTORIAN NOVELS
Copyright © 1997 by Natalie J. McKnight
ISBN 0-312-12295-0

Library of Congress Cataloging-in-Publication Data

McKnight, Natalie.
    Suffering mothers in mid-Victorian novels / by Natalie J.
McKnight.
        p. cm.
    Includes bibliographical references and index.
    ISBN 0-312-12295-0
    1. English fiction--19th century--History and criticism. 2. Women
and literature--Great Britain--History--19th century. 3. Mother and
child in literature. 4. Motherhood in literature. 5. Suffering in
literature. 6. Mothers in literature. I. Title.
PR878.M69M35 1996
823'.8093520431--dc20

                                                        96-34454
                                                        CIP

Book design by Milton Heiberg Studios

Printed in the United States of America by
Haddon Craftsmen
Scranton, PA

First Edition: January 1997

10 9 8 7 6 5 4 3 2 1

PERMISSIONS
The cover design was taken from a photograph of a Hablot Browne illus-
tration from one of the original monthly numbers of *Dombey and Son*. It
is called *A Chance Meeting,* and it appeared in number 13, October, 1847;
it is reproduced here by permission of the Rare Book Collection, Boston
University libraries.
        A briefer version of chapter 3 originally appeared in the December
1994 *Dickens Quarterly,* pages 177-86, and is reprinted here by permission of the Dickens Society.

For my parents

Contents

Acknowledgements

I would like to thank the staff of the Mugar Library at Boston University, particularly Charles Niles in Special Collections, for their cheerful and expert assistance in locating materials for my research. My thanks also go to the staffs of the Schlesinger and the Widener libraries at Harvard, the Boston Public Library, and Jo Meers at the Goucher College Library.

I am grateful to my friends and colleagues at Boston University, particularly Dean Brendan Gilbane, Linda Wells, Robert Wexelblatt, Mike Mahon, Eloise Knowlton, and John Fawell, for their support, suggestions, and especially humor, which helped to make the completion of this project possible.

I thank David Paroissien for permission to reprint parts of chapter 3, that appeared originally in *The Dickens Quarterly*. Michael Cotsell also deserves my thanks for his comments on my earliest drafts of chapter 3, which I presented on an MLA panel that he organized.

For their moral support and helpful comments, I thank my parents, George and Joanne Brown, and my friends, particularly Marge Betley, Mary Czymbor, and Judith Allen Ward. I am also grateful to my parents-in-law, Lee and Deborah McKnight, for their interest in my work and their willingness to discuss Victorian novels with me. To my husband, Jamie, and my daughters, Emily and Annie, I say thank you for rich mothering experiences that, in their variety, complexity, and joy, make the Victorian ideal seem rather wan in comparison.

Abbreviations

Works by Charlotte Brontë
JE   Jane Eyre
Pr   The Professor
Sh   Shirley
V   Villette

Works by Dickens
BH   Bleak House
BR   Barnaby Rudge
CC   A Christmas Carol
CS   Christmas Stories
DC   David Copperfield
D&S   Dombey and Son
GE   Great Expectations
HT   Hard Times
LD   Little Dorrit
MC   Martin Chuzzlewit
MED   The Mystery of Edwin Drood
NN   Nicholas Nickleby
OCS   The Old Curiosity Shop
OT   Oliver Twist
OMF   Our Mutual Friend
PP   The Pickwick Papers
TTC   A Tale of Two Cities
UT   The Uncommercial Traveller

Works by Eliot
AB   Adam Bede
DD   Daniel Deronda
FH   Felix Holt
MF   The Mill on the Floss
MM   Middlemarch

SCL   Scenes of Clerical Life
SM   Silas Marner

Works by Thackeray

HE   Henry Esmond
L   Lovel the Widower
P   Pendennis
VF   Vanity Fair
VR   Virginians

Suffering Mothers
in Mid-Victorian Novels

Chapter 1

Introduction to Suffering Mothers

When I first began studying the lives of Victorian women, I sympathized with the many women who suffered through the agonies of labor only to die shortly after the baby was delivered. As I continued my research, I began to feel more sympathy with those who survived childbirth. Early death was not necessarily the worst potential tragedy facing Victorian mothers. If they lived, they experienced relentless and impossible pressures and expectations, the traces of which linger in some present-day notions of motherhood. Conduct books for wives and mothers; popular periodical articles on motherhood; short stories, poems, and novels addressing motherhood; and medical guidebooks for mothers (nineteenth-century Dr. Spock books) proliferated in Victorian England, and all emphasized the awesome responsibilities of motherhood while defining mothering in increasingly complex, contradictory ways. New products on the market for mother and baby added to the onslaught of contradictory information middle-class mothers felt they had to master. What before had been a role considered fairly instinctual and natural was now becoming a task prescribed by doctors, manufacturers, writers, and early sociologists. The result of the proliferation of advice for mothers was often maternal confusion and frustration, physical threats to mother and child—sometimes even death—and almost always an exacerbation of what psychoanalysts consider the unavoidable guilt of mothers and frustrations of children directed against mothers. Children, their maternal fantasies fed by the popular cultural myths of ideal motherhood, wrote books as adults that reveal in intriguing, sometimes hidden patterns their peculiar ambivalence to mothers. Writers like Charles Dickens, George Eliot, Charlotte Brontë, and William Makepeace Thackeray particularly reward an analysis of mother figures in their novels. Since a comprehensive survey of mothers in Victorian fiction was beyond the scope of this book, I have chosen to focus primarily on major mid-Victorian authors. The works of these authors are exemplars of Victorian fiction, some of the most well-known and loved novels of the nineteenth century. The popularity of these writers' works in the nineteenth century suggests that they most likely reflected and affected current trends in mothering more than did most other fiction of their time.[1] Their novels offer insight into Victorian attitudes concerning motherhood, and the tensions surrounding mothers in these works help to explain their enduring fascination.

In *Myths of Motherhood: How Culture Reinvents the Good Mother,* Shari Thurer argues that twentieth-century mothers experience more angst over their roles than women of previous centuries did. "The current ideology of good mothering is not only spurious," Thurer claims, "it is oblivious of a mother's desires, limitations, and context, and when things go wrong, she tends to get blamed. This has resulted in a level of confusion and self-consciousness among mothers that their predecessors never knew."[2] I would argue, however, that the modern, self-conscious mother originated in Victorian England amidst a proliferation of mother-oriented publications, within a socioeconomic situation that increasingly limited and isolated women, and under a fecund queen whose public example established high standards for mothers. Victorian expectations of mothers still stick with us today in spite of the sexual revolution and the increase of women in the workplace. While women can work, most still feel compelled to meet standards of mothering that were impossibly high even when women were supposed to devote themselves almost exclusively to the care of husband and children. To gauge just how firmly Victorian standards for mothers have fixed themselves in our psyches all you need to do is try to get a class of college freshmen to sympathize with Nora Helmer when she walks out on her children in *A Doll's House* or with Edna Pontellier in *The Awakening* when she abandons her children by committing suicide; some students sympathize, of course, but many reveal a strong streak of hostility toward such untraditional moms. These texts invariably inspire the most hard-lined Victorian sentiments from many of my students: "A mother should live only for her children," "When a woman has a child she should no longer think of her own desires," etc. Victorian mores are alive and well in our culture.

To understand some of the origins of these mores and how they influence Victorian fiction, I'd like to examine in this chapter the advice that nineteenth-century conduct books and medical guidebooks offered to mothers, as well as the image of ideal motherhood created by articles, poems, and stories in Victorian periodicals and by Queen Victoria herself. The effect of this social context on the characterization of mothers in Victorian fiction will be suggested in general in the conclusion of this chapter and explored throughout the rest of the book.

I've entitled this work *Suffering Mothers in Mid-Victorian Novels* because many of the mother-characters I analyze do suffer inordinately throughout their respective narratives—physically, emotionally, socially, economically. Suffering seems to be the sine qua non of their existence, and at times authors, particularly Dickens, seem to enjoy inflicting the suffering on these characters. Mid-Victorian mothers often suffer because of their attempts and failures to live up to the maternal ideal. But I use the word "suffering" in another sense as well, for many of the maternal figures I examine must *be* suffered, or endured, by their families, friends, foes, and sometimes by the reader, too. Whether it's through their tyranny, their possessiveness, or their bathos, the mothers who must be suffered tend to be those who overplay certain aspects of the maternal ideal to the detriment of themselves and others.

Conduct Books for Women

Nineteenth-century conduct books for mothers provide the most obvious, if at times contradictory, picture of what was expected of mothers in Victorian England. The claims for and on mothers in these books are so excessive at times as to be laughable, when they are not downright exasperating. Granted, the reverence given to mothers in these writings is touching, but it helps to set up an ideal no woman could possibly reach, an ideal destined to create in most cases more guilt and frustration than good mothering. In *The Mothers of England: Their Influence and Responsibility,* published in 1844, Sarah Ellis, the nonmedical Benjamin Spock of her day, warns young women that "from the duties of a mother there is then no escape; and hence it follows, that if ever, in the whole course of women's life, she is called upon to think seriously it is when she first becomes a parent."[3] Ellis sees these "duties" as being nothing short of maintaining and developing the child's complete physical, mental, and spiritual health, pretty much without the help of father. It is the mother who must "cultivate the mind—the immortal nature of her child," Ellis claims.[4] Sarah Lewis in *Woman's Mission,* published in 1840, stresses mothers' spiritual role even more forcefully. She points out that women were the " 'last at the cross, and the first at the sepulchre' " and from this biblical precedent derives the conclusion that women have "no less an office than that of instruments (under God) for the regeneration of the world,—restorers of God's image in the human soul."[5] Isabella Beeton, in her oft-reprinted *Mrs. Beeton's Household Management* (originally published in installments in 1859-60), concurs with Ellis and Lewis, stating that with the mother "rests not only the care for the daily needs of food, clothing and the like of her children, but, what is even more important, their moral training." And no one can accomplish this training better than the mother, Beeton asserts, although she does not explain why, except to suggest that the knowledge about how to raise children seems to arrive naturally with the birth of the child.[6] Of course Beeton's book, as its name suggests, focuses more on the more mundane issues of household management and less on mothering, which partly explains her vagueness when it comes to advice.

In general, these authors elevate attitudes toward the role of mothering, forcefully arguing that it is not a minor function for second-class citizens but is in fact the most important job imaginable. At the same time, the implication in these books is that any intellectual or spiritual failing in the child can and should be attributed to the mother. Lewis asserts that women "as the guardian angels of man's infancy are charged with a mission—to them is committed the implanting of that heavenly germ to which God must indeed give the increase; but for the early culture of which they are answerable."[7] The father is scarcely ever mentioned in any of these works. Beyond his role as breadwinner, he seems to have had little responsibility in childrearing. Ellis regrets that fathers do not play a larger role in the home because they for the most part are too involved in business affairs, but she does not argue that men should change their schedules or that the business world should be altered to encourage fathers to spend more time with their families; instead she assumes the male world is unalterable, "and therefore it becomes more the duty of mothers, especially those of the middle class of society . . . to inquire earnestly into the probable means of ensuring the future good of their children." After all, the mother is "*the* person whose influence over [the children] is the most powerful . . . she is *the* person into whose hands their mental and spiritual welfare is placed."[8]

If Ellis, Lewis, or Beeton had reasonable advice as to how to shape a child's intellect and soul, their claims would be less frustrating, but in fact the advice they do give often seems vague, contradictory, or shockingly at odds with the nature of children. Mrs. Beeton had four children and died shortly after the birth of the fourth, but one can tell that Ellis had little or no hands-on parenting experience, particularly when reading her confident proclamations concerning the disciplining of children. She believes that the mother should institute from the child's infancy onward a method of "requiring obedience to the parent's wishes, simply as such, accompanied by a strict regard to clearness, consistency, and truth, in making those wishes known." She continues, "to a child trained up in this manner, obedience is so easy, that it no more thinks of questioning the mother's right to direct its actions, than it quarrels with the nurse because she stretches out her arms to prevent its falling."[9] In reading this, mothers could not help but feel that either they are particularly bad parents or have unusually uncooperative children. Ellis's advice seems designed to make mothers dissatisfied with both themselves and their children, for few if any children obey their parents so consistently and easily unless driven to obedience by fear. Even if one knew Ellis never had children of her own (which was the case), a parent's natural response to her confident assessment of discipline would be to feel guilty and inadequate since one's own children never respond to discipline so obediently. And since the Victorian mother was being told that she alone was responsible for the child's behavior, she had to bear the guilt by herself. Never once does Ellis admit that there will be times when a child is completely unmanageable and moments when any normal mother will want to bang her head against hard objects in sheer frustration.

As Sally Shuttleworth points out in "Demonic Mothers: Ideologies of Bourgeois Motherhood in the Mid-Victorian Era," "motherhood was set at the ideological centre of the Victorian bourgeois ideal," and ideals of motherhood helped to establish and perpetuate gender and class hierarchies by solidifying rigid divisions of labor between men and women of the middle class.[10] Lower class women who had to work had no hope of upholding the middle-class ideal of motherhood. Because of this heavy ideological burden, Shuttleworth suggests, motherhood was subjected to what Michel Foucault describes as surveillance and discipline perhaps more stringently than any other aspect of middle-class life. Motherhood was the cornerstone of the social structure and therefore had to be controlled at all costs. The cost, of course, was usually paid by the mothers themselves.

In *The Women of England: Their Social Duties and Domestic Habits,* published in 1843, Ellis laid burdens of guilt on women in general, not just mothers, with her excessive expectations and contradictory advice. At the beginning of the day, according to Ellis, women should not ask themselves " 'what shall I do to gratify myself—to be admired—or to vary the tenor of my existence?' " Instead they should ask,

> "how shall I endeavor through this day to turn the time, the health, and the means permitted me to enjoy, to the best ac- count?—Is any one sick? I must visit their chamber without de- lay. . . . Is any one about to set off on a journey? I must see that the early meal is spread, or prepare it with my own hands, in order that the servant, who was working late last night, may profit by unbroken rest. Did I fail in what was kind or consider- ate to any of the family yesterday?"[11]

As if her demands for self-erasure were not obvious enough, Ellis spells them out again a few pages later, when she writes that a woman needs to be told that it is necessary

> to lay aside all her natural caprice, her love of self-indulgence, her vanity, her indolence—in short, her very *self*—and assum- ing a new nature, which nothing less than watchfulness and prayer can enable her constantly to maintain, to spend her men- tal and moral capabilities in devising means for promoting the happiness of others, while her own derives a remote and sec- ondary existence from theirs.[12]

She could not more clearly indicate that women, and particularly wives and mothers, should have no existence separate from their duties and affections toward their families and communities. As if this advice were not difficult enough to follow, Ellis ends the book with the warning that it is "*mistaken* kindness" for a woman to allow herself to become a "house- hold drudge."[13] In other words, women should devote their every wak- ing moment to working for others but somehow not turn into drudges in the process. Just how a woman is to pull off this performance is not clarified by Ellis. Perhaps if she sings and whistles while she works like Snow White she can be both productive and entertaining at the same time. What is amazing about Ellis's books is their supreme self-confidence; she dishes out her advice without any hesitancy. Reading her works 150 years after they were written, with a healthy dose of skepticism and a critical eye, I still found myself feeling thoroughly inadequate as a mother. Realizing how absurd and unrealistic her advice often is did not prevent me from measuring my own acts against it, probably because the Victorian image of the ideal selfless mother still tenaciously clings to our psyches, as Shari Thurer has argued.[14] If a twentieth-century woman finds herself vulnerable to Ellis's expectations, imagine the reaction of typical middle-class Victorian mothers.

In *The Wives of England* (1843), Ellis almost self-destructs under the tensions of her contradictions. She advises that a woman should never become a slave in her home and that she should never give up what she is unwilling to give up, nor withhold what she is expected to give. To determine what they must give and withhold, Ellis suggests that women use this rule, "that none should give up more than they are prepared to resign without grudging, whether noticed and appreciated or not."[15] So if a woman thinks that she might feel resentment or expect appreciation for her sacrifice, Ellis indicates that she should not make it. Yet 20 pages later, Ellis returns to her appeal to women to abandon their own feelings and to meet marital trials "by an habitual subjection of self to the interests and happiness of others."[16] In other words, women should not sacrifice if the sacrifice will make them feel resentful, but they should not be feeling resentful to begin with, so they should make the sacrifice. Considering the popularity of Ellis's conduct books in England and America, the confusion and frustration felt by women from this source alone must have been widespread.

Sarah Lewis sets up a similarly frustrating contradiction in *Woman's Mission*. She argues for complete unselfishness in mothers, believing that mothers should devote themselves to the mental and spiritual development of their children. Yet, at the same time, according to Lewis, mothers should not allow themselves to become dull. They should cultivate their intellect for the sake of their children, particularly their sons, otherwise their sons will be bored with them and lose respect for them as they grow older: "here, I may observe, is a great inducement for mothers to cultivate their intellectual powers, for those powers will materially affect their influence over grown-up sons."[17] Women, then, should continue to develop their minds, not for their own sakes, not for the enrichment of their own lives, but as part of their maternal duty to their sons. She argues that since women were meant " 'to live for others' " the cultivation of their intellect should be for others, and she adamantly proclaims that women should never be educated to enter the public sphere, for then maternal duties would be considered less and less important and would be relegated to those least able to fulfill them.[18] Just how one is supposed to be completely selfless but still maintain a self that a grown-up son would be interested in is a problem that Lewis does not address in detail. And, like Ellis, in the midst of these puzzling paradoxes, she makes proclamations that seem designed to create feelings of guilt and inadequacy, such as her assertion that good mothers should be able to counteract any negative influence of society on their children. It's a lovely idea, of course, but not one that has much relation to reality. Lewis's book exalts the role of mother as second to none, and it is refreshing at least in its focus on the need for women to continue to cultivate their mental powers throughout their lives. But its call for maternal self-abnegation is relentless.

As Patricia Branca points out in *Silent Sisterhood: Middle Class Women in the Victorian Home,* the intensive care that Victorian mothers were asked to give to their children was particularly demanding in light of the number of children many women had: "If the Victorian woman continued to have the traditional number of children, it would be virtually impossible to implement the changes in childrearing because they demanded increased and elaborate care for each and every child." The excessive demands on mothers throughout the nineteenth-century, Branca indicates, led to a gradual decrease in the birthrate.[19]

Medical Guidebooks

Medical guidebooks and other medical publications in the Victorian era similarly confused, oppressed, and produced guilt in mothers. Patricia Branca has noted that "according to most of the authorities on the subject of infant care, the mother's mis-management of the child was largely to blame for the thousands of unfortunate deaths."[20] Branca quotes an article published in *The British Mothers' Journal* in June of 1858 that basically calls mothers murderers:

> "On [mothers'] shoulders lies the greater part of the blame [for infant mortality]—*we* fill the churchyards, and send babies a short cut from the cradle to the grave—we kill them by our bad management. Almost every baby comes into the world quite strong and healthy enough to live long and to have good health; it is *we* who cut life short, just as truly as we cut off tape with our scissors. . . . Yes, women have been in the world six thousand years, and still up to this very day we do not know how to manage our little ones!"[21]

Advertisements for Dr. Alfred Fennings' book on child care (1856) echoed this sentiment: " 'Do not let your children die. Fennings' *Every Mother's Book* contains everything a mother ought to know about her child's feed-

ing, teething, sleeping, weaning, also Hints, cautions, remedies for all dis-
eases. . . . save your child's life by reading it.' "[22] Mothers who had just lost
children and who hadn't read Dr. Fennings' book would be set up by his
advertisement to agonize about whether their own failure to keep up
with the latest child-care experts had resulted in their babies' deaths. Dr.
Thomas Bull, another child-care expert, was also explicit in his blame,
stating that even " 'one act of disobedience' " to medical advice could
ruin a woman's "hope of success" in her pregnancy.[23]

These texts not only exacerbated maternal guilt, but also often dis-
seminated bad advice. In 1842, Dr. Bull in his *Hints to Mothers, for the
Management of Health During the Period of Pregnancy, and in the Lying-
in-Room; with an Exposure of Popular Errors in Connexion with Those Subjects,* promoted some popular errors of his own. Consider his statement
that women don't need to eat any more than usual during pregnancy
since most people already eat more than they need to. Pregnant women
trying to follow that advice would have experienced some serious hunger pangs and probably would have deprived their babies and themselves of necessary nourishment. He also advises that if a woman's breasts
get too swollen during pregnancy she should have applied to them "half
a dozen leeches, or more."[24]

Bull was a master of laying on the guilt. Most women, he believed,
could prevent miscarriages, if they were just careful enough. "Delicacy of
constitution, connected with habits of indulgence" could lead to miscarriage, Bull warned.[25] And any woman susceptible to miscarriage or of a
delicate constitution in general should sleep alone from the time of conception—"this is absolutely and imperatively necessary," he commands.[26]
One of the numerous problems with this advice is that most women
could not determine the moment of conception. In fact, many women
could not really verify their pregnancies until the point of quickening—
when the fetal movements could be felt, around the fifth month of pregnancy. Cessation of menstruation was not an adequate predictor as poor
diet, fatigue, stress, and numerous illnesses could cause amenorrhea.
Cessation of menstruation combined with morning sickness would be a
fairly convincing indicator, but many women do not get morning sickness. Not only would it be difficult to determine pregnancy in the early
months, but even if one could, it would be difficult for any middle-class
Victorian woman, conditioned in obedience, meekness, and silence, to
tell her husband that their sexual relations would have to cease. So, in
effect, Dr. Bull tells women that they have the power to prevent miscarriages if they follow his advice but his advice would have been impossible

to follow. Shuttleworth describes how most of the medical texts during this time period established similar frustrating contradictions so that "obedience . . . seemed almost designed as a deliberate impossibility: a pregnant woman should take exercise but not too much, rest but not be idle, take cold baths but refrain from catching cold." Shuttleworth concludes that "all the rules seemed calculated to drive her into that very state of anxiety which she was warned was fatal, and a clear result of her own weakness and disobedience."[27]

Dr. Bull did offer some useful advice in his book, however. He warned against using calomel for bowel problems because it had mercury in it. He also warned against the use of opiates, which were a common feature of nurseries in the form of "laudanum, sirup of white poppies, Dolby's carminative, and Godfrey's cordial."[28] Useful to the nurse, these opiates were often fatal to infants; Bull describes two cases of infants dying of convulsions after having been administered Godfrey's cordial.[29] Bull's mention of specific brand names indicates that these products were probably well-known and in common use. Women probably felt compelled, as good, modern mothers, to purchase the latest products on the market for their babies' ease, not knowing that some of these products could prove absolutely fatal. Teething was one of the top ten causes of death in young children because opiate syrups were administered to them to soothe their pain and keep them calm. Too much syrup and the child would overdose, convulse, and die.[30] A scene in Vanity Fair illustrates the divergent beliefs about administering soothing syrups to babies. Amelia discovers her mother in the act of giving baby Georgy "Daffy's Elixir" to quiet his cries. After Amelia has "flung the bottle crashing into the fireplace," saying, " 'I will not have baby poisoned, mamma,' " she explains that their doctor said that the elixir was poisonous, and, taking offense, Mrs. Sedley replies, " 'Very good: you think I'm a murderess then. . . . This is the language you use to your mother' " (VF 455). According to J. I. M. Stewart in his notes to the Penguin edition, "poison" was probably too harsh a word for the concoction, but the elixir did contain gin, not an uncommon ingredient in soothing medications for infants and young children.[31]

Shari Thurer shows how in the twentieth century the invasion of doctors into the role of mothering has often produced some negative results; many of her conclusions apply to the effect of doctors on nineteenth-century mothering as well. First, the overall effect of making mothering scientific was to make women dependent on child-care authorities, thereby taking mothering away from women and handing the role over to men. Second, these authorities were often spouting advice that was wrongheaded and wronghearted (which has been the case in the twentieth century as well—Thurer cites the American Children's Bureau's *Infant Care,* which in the early twentieth century advised that parents should not play with their babies for fear of overstimulating them).[32]

But doctors' intrusions on nineteenth-century mothering often produced more direct negative effects. As Patricia Branca points out, women suffered by switching from midwives to doctors for childbirth, because the rate of deaths from puerperal fever increased, probably due to the fact that doctors carried germs from previous diseased patients to the scenes of birth. Midwives, who did not deal with sick patients, were less likely to spread disease. Middle-class women made up the majority of victims, since they were the ones to switch to doctors in the greatest numbers.[33] Even when doctors weren't outright killing their female patients, they were often not helping much either. Victorian prudishness cast its pall on the medical profession, resulting in doctors who were afraid to touch their female patients except in the final stage of delivery. Doctors even resisted applying stethoscopes to the abdomen to hear the fetal heartbeat. Dr. Henry Allbut dismissed prudery in the 1880s when he published *The Wife's Handbook: How A Woman Should Order Herself During Pregnancy,* which told women they could determine if they were pregnant by examining their vaginas using a mirror—if the vaginal passage had a violet color, they were pregnant. For his forthrightness in casting aside prudery, Dr. Allbut was cast out of the British Medical Register, having offended the register's more traditional doctors.[34]

Periodicals and Other Sources

Medical and behavioral guidebooks for women were certainly not the only cultural influence on Victorian mothers. Periodicals frequently turned to the subject of mothering in articles, short stories, poems, and serialized novels. And as I will show in subsequent chapters, characterizations of mothers in major Victorian novels naturally were shaped by and helped to shape the expectations of mothers in general. The dominant tone of the periodical pieces devoted to mothers is perhaps captured best by Andrew Halliday's article "Mothers" in Dickens's periodical *All the Year Round,* September 9, 1865. "Some one has said, that a young mother is the most beautiful thing in nature," Halliday opens, but "why qualify it? Why young? Are not all mothers beautiful?" He progresses from this opening to increasingly overblown adulation, comparing maternal love to "a holy passion" and "a sacred flame on the altar of the heart" and stating that a mother is the "mainspring of all nature, the fountain of all pure love." Having exulted mothers this much, the only way he can increase his praise is by comparing mothers to God, which he straightaway does. Mothers are "the first likeness on earth of God himself."[35] Toward the end of the article one finds Halliday's motivation for praising mothers so exuberantly: he finds their lot in life so miserable that he sees them as martyrs. He states that novelists are wise to end most novels at the point of marriage for that might be the last chance for a happy ending—after that event women's misery begins. Only maternal love prevents their lives from being solely miserable; "no man knows what a woman suffers in bearing and bringing up a family of children. Only Heaven knows— Heaven which has endowed her with that wondrous love which redeems her existence from being an intolerable slavery."[36] Such hyperbolic praise of mothers often accompanies a keen awareness of their suffering in the writings of Victorian authors; numerous passages in Thackeray—particularly ones I will quote in chapter 5 referring to Amelia Sedley and her suffering in *Vanity Fair* and Helen Pendennis's angelic devotion in *Pendennis*—reflect similar attitudes and concerns. One gets the impression that these men want to compensate women for their miseries by giving them excessive verbal praise—but notice that neither man suggests giving them anything but praise. No revision of the conditions of mothers' lives is even suggested.

Leigh Hunt adopts a similar reverential tone in his poem "Childbed: A Prose Poem," published in the *Monthly Repository* in 1837. He lauds the beauty and martyrdom of mothers, and in the final stanza of the prose poem, he offers a sentimental picture of the devoted husband paying tribute to his wife after labor:

> It was on a May evening , in a cottage flowering with the green-gage, in the time of hyacinths and new hopes, when the hand that wrote this, took the hand that had nine times lain thin and delicate on the bed of a mother's endurance; and he kissed it, like a bride's.[37]

Of course, Hunt seems to be paying tribute not only to his wife's endurance but also to his own sweet devotion to her. It is difficult to ascertain which moves him more. And he neglects to mention that her hand was probably so thin and delicate not just because of the rigors of pregnancy and labor but also because he was habitually insolvent.

Sarah Ellis's long moral tale, *First Impressions; Or, Hints to Those Who Would Make Home Happy* (1849), presents another paean to motherhood. Owen Meredith, a curate and the protagonist of the tale, ritually performs homage to his mother every Sunday, as if she were a maternal deity. He takes out her picture on the Sabbath, feeling that it is "too sacred to be generally exposed" on the weekdays, and "suspending it over his mantel-piece, would sit and gaze on it, until the mute image seemed to glow again with life."[38] Ellis prefigures Sigmund Freud in her observations of such idolizing devotion to a mother. The narrator describes how Owen's gaze on his mother's picture at times profanes it by comparing her loveliness to the features of another attractive woman he saw that day, suggesting his interest is not merely filial. But he takes great offense if anyone else looks at her in a sexual light. Squire Allonby comments about the picture of Owen's mother, saying, " 'A figure like that would most probably grow more lusty in middle life,' " and Owen sternly replies, " 'My mother never was lusty, sir.' "[39] How much of this Ellis intended to be funny is difficult to determine, probably none of it as humor hardly seems her forte. It is likely that Ellis introduces this scene of a son's reverence for his mother in order to show Owen's high character in general and filial devotion in particular so the reader can continue to sympathize with him later in the tale when he develops a serious drinking problem. Having shown his dedication to an ideal mother, he can sustain some sins without losing all reader sympathy. And the image of an ideal mother is easy to sustain here because the mother is safely buried and therefore can only be scrutinized through the haze of memory.

Eliza Lynn, in a *Household Words* story called "A Mother," takes a slightly more realistic look at motherhood. The mother in her story has the best intentions—she is a widow and tackles the difficulties of single parenthood with vigilance and diligence. She wants to raise her son well, has the best intentions, tries very hard, but ultimately fails—mostly, Lynn implies, because she pampered the boy too much as a child, keeping him from the corrupting influence of other boys and studies that might not be good for him. When he goes to university, he resents his pampered upbringing, which had brought him to "an ignorant and ridiculous manhood."[40] The mother's protectiveness results in a son ill-equipped to deal with the temptations of his new life, and he falls into a debauched lifestyle (a pattern similar to that seen in Thackeray's *Pendennis,* in which the spoiled Arthur goes off to college and is ruined). Her second failing is her deficiency in affection. She treats him coldly when he becomes dissipated and has too much pride to "entreat, to caress," actions which, she realizes later, might have had a positive effect.[41] The story concludes with her paying off his debts but changing her name and leaving the country to avoid the shame he has brought on her. In this story, Lynn seems to be upholding the high standards of the guidebooks for women, implying that a mother's good intentions, dedication, and vigilance are not enough— a mother must also be both wise and ever warm and forgiving for the relationship to be successful. Lynn also concurs with the guidebooks in her conclusion that if anything goes wrong with the child, it must be the mother's fault. The mother narrates the story and takes the blame for the son's faults fully upon herself.

The reverence shown to mothers and the expectations of them demonstrated in these pieces ally them with the works of Ellis, Lewis, and Beeton in perpetuating the belief that it is a mother's role to suffer all for her family and that she should be happy to do so for the respect it will bring to her. The gentle, mild, long-suffering, devoted, and voiceless mother depicted in these works is akin to the Virgin Mary, the ultimate mother, the standard no woman can live up to but to whom Victorian women, at least, were compared. Halliday, in fact, bemoans the fact that in Protestant countries mothers are not as revered because the Virgin is not as emphasized as in Catholic countries.[42] But it seems that the predominating Protestantism of England did not stop the Virgin Mother from being the ultimate reference for good mothering.

Queen Victoria

Second only to the Virgin Mother in her influence on Victorian expectations of motherhood was Queen Victoria. As a mother of nine, and as the sovereign of England, she became an emblem of the ideal mother— fertile; patient; long-suffering in her labors; devoted to her husband, children, and country; and very traditional in her public attitudes about the roles of men and women. Her "iron will" helped her to keep up her ideal image in spite of the reality of her feelings toward sex, pregnancy, and motherhood.[43] Queen Victoria perpetuated the gap between the ideal and the real that conduct books for mothers had developed. The public perceived her as a strong, contented mother, but in private Victoria actually expressed startlingly negative sentiments about motherhood, particularly in letters to her daughters when they became adults. She counseled her daughter Vicky that bearing children "was not only dangerous and agonising, but 'a complete violence to all one's feelings of propriety (which God knows receive a shock enough in marriage alone).' "[44] The remark implies, of course, that next to sexual intercourse, childbearing is the worse of two evils. " 'No girl could go to the altar if she knew all,' " she asserted.[45] Queen Victoria apparently found the sexual act so alienating that she felt women had no real part in conceiving—the production of children was all men's fault, she states in a letter to Vicky, dated March 9, 1859:

> It is indeed too hard and dreadful what we have to go through and men ought to have an adoration for one, and indeed to do every thing to make up, for what after all they alone are the cause of! I must say it is a bad arrangement, but we must calmly, patiently bear it, and feel that we can't help it and therefore we must forget it, and the more we retain our pure, modest feelings, the easier it is to get over it all afterwards.[46]

For the queen, sex and labor were the heaviest crosses of women's martyrdom. But not only did the queen feel squeamish about sexual intercourse, ambivalent about conception, and horrified by childbirth, but she also loathed the nine months in-between, was depressed after pregnancy, and was not very fond of the idea of babies to begin with. She felt pregnancy had " 'utterly spoiled' " her first two years of marriage; " 'I could enjoy nothing,' " she asserted, " 'not travel about or go about with dear Papa.' "[47] She felt her wings were " 'clipped' " by pregnancy, and when in later life she would learn of a daughter's or granddaughter's pregnancy she called the information " 'horrid news.' "[48] The experience of giving birth made her feel " 'like a cow or a dog,' " and after it was over she often experienced terrible depressions.[49] In a letter dated February 23, 1859, the queen tells Vicky to expect "lowness and tendency to cry" after giving birth—"it is what every lady suffers with more or less and what I, during my two first confinements, suffered dreadfully with."[50] Perhaps one reason that pregnancy and childbirth were so miserable for her was because she did not particularly like the idea of babies. "I hated the thought of having children," she wrote to Vicky on March 16, 1859, "and have no adoration for very little babies (particularly not in their baths till they are past 3 or 4 months.)"[51]

In short, Queen Victoria was hardly the patient, uncomplaining, natural mother enamored of little babies and fulfilled by the experience of becoming a mother. She was not what the guidebooks said mothers should be. Yet she successfully projected that image to the public, thereby inspiring and furthering the expectations of mothers established by guidebooks, periodicals, and novels. Sarah Ellis in *The Women of England: Their Social Duties and Domestic Habits* posits the young Queen Victoria as an ideal for all English women and lauds her as a great influence on the high moral character of English women and a reason why their moral influence in society should grow.[52] Ellis dedicates *The Wives of England* to "Her Majesty the Queen, In whose exalted station the social virtues of domestic life present the brightest example to her countrywomen, and the surest presage of her empire's glory."[53] Clearly Ellis was not privy to the queen's more caustic remarks on motherhood. The queen's bitter comments about the horrors of pregnancy and childbirth and men's responsibility in both sound more (in tone) like the fumings of Dickens's acerbic Miss Wade in *Little Dorrit,* and the queen's antipathy toward little babies seems in the same league as the unmotherly Sally Brass in *The Old Curiosity Shop.* In effect, the queen's very understandable, realistic feelings about motherhood are so far from the accepted ideal of the time that they would place her in the ranks of the villains in the novelistic world. This says a lot about the grossly unrealistic portrayal and expectations of mothers in Victorian novels, portrayals shaped by all of the influences above including Queen Victoria herself.

Reality vs. Fiction

Another reality check to the Victorian maternal ideal is provided by statistics that show an increase in infanticide in the early to mid-Victorian age—1834 to 1844—probably due to hardships caused by Poor Laws that made it extremely difficult for single mothers to get financial support.[54] With no help to turn to, women like George Eliot's Hetty Sorrel were driven to kill their own babies, a historical fact that perhaps Newt Gingrich should review. Medical doctors tried to explain infanticide by blaming it on insanity caused by puerperal fever, the assumption being that no sane woman could act in such an unmaternal fashion. Blaming uncontrollable physical forces for such behavior protected the ideal of Victorian motherhood while admitting the reality of infanticide. According to Carol Smart in "Disruptive Bodies and Unruly Sex: The Regulation of Reproduction and Sexuality in the Nineteenth Century," the rates of infanticide only began to decrease when the rates of abortion increased: "women were beginning to favour terminations over neglectful or active infanticide."[55]

Baby farming was another negative reality of some classes of Victorian mothers, but one often unacknowledged by the guidebooks, periodical writers, and novelists. Women charged low fees to take care of babies and many then neglected them, sometimes so completely as to lead to infant deaths. Becky in *Vanity Fair* farms out little Rawdon Crawley and seldom visits him, but Thackeray shows that the nurse who is bought for him is probably more affectionate than Becky ever would have been.

Other babies were not so lucky. Smart discusses the case of Margaret Waters, who was tried in 1870 for the death of four babies who were in her care. Hers was not an isolated case, and advertisements for such farms were common in the newspapers. Baby farming was a necessary evil for the lower-class woman who needed to work and had little or no support from her child's father or her family. By 1872 the Act for the Protection of Infant Life was instituted to monitor such establishments; still the feeling prevailed that women who tried to work and raise children were bad mothers.[56]

No female character in a novel could farm out her baby and still be considered good; no mother character could even admit to not liking babies, as Queen Victoria had, and still be considered good; nor could any get away with complaining about childbearing to the extent that the queen does in her letters. There was simply little or no acceptance of these unavoidable situations and natural feelings among the general public, or at least novelists seemed to think so. Good mothers in Victorian novels either have babies without complaining and care for them devotedly or die quietly and without complaining in childbirth, like poor Mrs. Dombey in *Dombey and Son*. Good mothers dote on their infants: an example of this is Celia in *Middlemarch,* who, granted, is depicted as rather silly in her all-consuming devotion to her baby, but the portrayal is certainly affectionate. Portrayals of mothers in Dickens's novels tend either to reflect and further the ideal promulgated by guidebooks—the angel—or to depict bitch mothers: monsters of selfishness, who are unable or unwilling to express love to their children. Brontë's and Eliot's mothers are subtler mixes of positive and destructive characteristics and strengths and flaws, while Thackeray's are often extreme conjunctions of both angel and monster. Certainly Victorian novelistic characterizations of mothers are not all dull stereotypes. The longing and wish-fulfillment apparent in the angels, and the hostility and vindictiveness vented in the characterizations of bitch mothers—and the confusion apparent in the characterizations that are both—make these mothers fascinating subjects to study. These characters reveal the terrible tensions created by impossible social expectations of mothers, expectations that not only put mothers at a disadvantage but also set up children for disappointment, even a sense of victimization when they compared their own female parent to the ideal. Mother characters in Victorian novels, then, reveal current social norms of motherhood but also reveal intriguing aspects of the novelists' psyches, and sometimes our own, as I hope to show throughout this study. This longing for the perfect mother and blaming of the imperfect mother is most obvious in the works of Dickens and Thackeray; Brontë and Eliot seem to find more middle ground between the two extremes, probably because as women they were closer to understanding the realities of motherhood and the discrepancies between the realities and prevailing expectations, even though they were never biological mothers themselves. They were less likely to long for the impossible ideal, then, or cast blame for the shortcomings of mothers.

Beside the less extreme, more mixed mothers of Brontë and Eliot, the other main alternative to the angel or bitch mothers is the absent mother. Mothers are missing to a startling degree in Victorian fiction. Granted, the prevalence of missing mothers in novels reflects the very real threat of death in delivery or from puerperal fever. Novelists, in part, were capturing the life-threatening reality of motherhood in the nineteenth century by showing how often mothers simply were not on hand to watch their children mature. But the frequency of death in childbirth cannot completely explain the absence of mother figures or the resistance of most novelists to follow their female protagonists past marriage and into motherhood. It seems that mothers are often missing in these works because the complex of emotions surrounding the idea of mother and the contradictory and impossible expectations of mothers make these creatures something better left out of the story because of the confusion and antipathy they inspire. They may be too hot a commodity to handle, or at least to handle too often or too closely. But even their absence is a presence. As Sally Shuttleworth argues, absent mothers often have more influence in Victorian fiction than do present ones, so that "motherhood is simultaneously marginalized and given ideological centrality."[57] Mothers' absence in numerous novels creates a vacuum that destabilizes the protagonists and therefore incites their development and the action of the novels in general. Without the protection and guidance of a mother, heroines can assert their independence and adventurousness more freely. Both Brontë and Eliot use the absence of mothers strategically in several of their novels, as I shall show.

When present, the mother in Victorian novels is often the locus for overcharged yearnings, resentments, and disappointments and the convergence of complex and contradictory expectations—or she is a two-dimensional reflection of popular guidebooks. When she is absent, her absence becomes a great motivator and instigator. She is the great creator that must be tamed and contained by characters and novelists, doctors and guidebooks, periodicals and royalty alike. She is all-important, Victorian ideology asserted, but she better not try to be too important.

Notes

1. Obviously an analysis of mothers in works by novelists such as Elizabeth Gaskell, Emily and Anne Brontë, Wilkie Collins, and others would also be worthwhile. Pauline Nestor's *Female Friendships and Communities* offers interesting insights into this area of Gaskell's works (as well as Charlotte Brontë's and George Eliot's).

2. Shari L. Thurer, *The Myths of Motherhood: How Culture Reinvents the Good Mother* (Boston: Houghton Mifflin, 1994), xii.

3. Sarah Ellis, *The Mothers of England: Their Influence and Responsibility* (New York: D. Appleton & Co., 1844), 9.

4. Ibid., 15.

5. Sarah Lewis, *Woman's Mission* (Boston: William Crosby & Co. 1840), 9, 11.

6. Isabella Beeton, *Mrs. Beeton's Household Management,* Rev. ed. (London: Ward, Lock & Co., 1949), 1621, 1624.

7. Lewis, 30.

8. Ellis, *The Mothers of England,* 66, 42.

9. Ibid., 22.

10. Sally Shuttleworth, "Demonic Mothers: Ideologies of Bourgeois Motherhood in the Mid-Victorian Era," in *Rewriting the Victorians: Theory, History, and the Politics of Gender,* ed. Linda M. Shires (New York: Routledge, 1992), 31-32.

11. Sarah Ellis, *The Women of England: Their Social Duties and Domestic Habits* (New York: J. & H. G. Langley, 1843), 9.

12. Ibid., 15.

13. Ibid., 74.

14. Thurer, 185.

15. Sarah Ellis, *The Wives of England: Their Relative Duties, Domestic Influence and Social Obligations* (New York: Langley, 1843), 33.

16. Ibid., 55.

17. Lewis, 33.

18. Ibid., 51, 46.

19. Patricia Branca, *Silent Sisterhood: Middle Class Women in the Victorian Home* (Pittsburgh: Carnegie-Mellon University Press, 1975), 112.

20. Ibid., 99.

21. Ibid.

22. Quoted in Ibid., 96.

23. Quoted in Shuttleworth, 138.

24. Thomas Bull, *Hints to Mothers, for the Management of Health During the Period of Pregnancy, and in the Lying-in-Room; with an Exposure of Popular*

Errors in Connexion with those Subjects, 3rd ed. (New York, Wiley and Putnam, 1842), 23-24, 88.

25. Ibid., 103.

26. Ibid., 114-15.

27. Shuttleworth, 38.

28. Bull, 228.

29. Ibid., 229.

30. Branca, 98.

31. William Makepeace Thackeray, *Vanity Fair,* ed. J. I. M. Stewart (New York: Penguin, 1985), 808.

32. Thurer, 235.

33. Branca, 86, 89; Thurer, 200.

34. Branca, 83-84.

35. Andrew Halliday, "Mothers," *All the Year Round,* Sept. 9, 1865, 157.

36. Ibid., 159.

37. Leigh Hunt, "Childbed: A Prose Poem," *Monthly Repository* new enlarged series, 1 (1837): 356.

38. Sarah Ellis, *First Impressions; Or, Hints to Those Who Would Make Home Happy* (New York: Appleton, 1849), 10.

39. Ibid., 16.

40. Eliza Lynn, "A Mother," *Household Words,* April 4, 1857: 333.

41. Lynn, 334.

42. Halliday, 158.

43. Giles St. Aubyn, *Queen Victoria* (New York: Atheneum, 1992), 161.

44. Quoted in Ibid., 159.

45. Quoted in Ibid., 159.

46. *Dearest Child: Letters Between Queen Victoria and the Princess Royal 1858-61,* ed. Roger Fulford (New York: Holt, Rinehart and Winston, 1964), 165.

47. Quoted in St. Aubyn, 159.

48. Quoted in Ibid., 159.

49. Quoted in Ibid., 160.

50. *Dearest Child,* 162.

51. *Dearest Child,* 167.

52. Ellis, *The Women of England,* 20.

53. Ellis, *The Wives of England,* dedication page.

54. Carol Smart, "Disruptive Bodies and Unruly Sex: The Regulation of Reproduction and Sexuality in the Nineteenth Century," *Regulating Wom-*

anhood: Historical Essays on Marriage, Motherhood and Sexuality (New York: Routledge, 1992), 17.

55. Ibid., 18.
56. Ibid., 23.
57. Shuttleworth, 44.

Chapter 2

Mothering Theory and Miserable or Missing Mothers in Victorian Novels

The expectations of mothers created through nineteenth-century guide books and periodicals, the image that Queen Victoria projected, and the other influences discussed in chapter 1 help to explain the tensions that accrue around mother characters in Victorian novels and between Victorian authors and their mothers. The expectations were extreme and ubiquitous, setting children and parents up for certain disappointment. But these influences certainly were not the only factor in creating ambivalence toward mothers. Psychoanalytic mothering theories suggest that even a perfect mother (if one were possible) probably would inspire hostile feelings in her children. The problems stem from the traditional family dynamic, with a mother at home as primary caregiver (with the help, sometimes, of other females such as governesses and nannies) and a father who works outside the home and devotes less time and attention to the children. This structure was typical of nineteenth-century middle-class families and holds true in many cases today. In fact psychologists help to perpetuate this family structure as the norm by using for most of their studies mothers who stay home with their children while the fathers leave to go to work. By limiting their studies in this manner,

psychologists reaffirm "popularly accepted notions about the circumstances in which motherhood should occur."[1] Today, even with a high
percentage of mothers working, mothers are still, in general, devoting
more time to the care of children than are fathers: " 'shared parenting'
[has] remained a pipe dream in most households," Shari Thurer states.[2]
(This inequality can be seen in other areas of responsibility around the
home. In spite of the fact that today almost 70 percent of educated women
with young children work outside the home, women are "still doing 84
percent of the housework.")[3] The dominance of mothers in the home
situates them as the prime target of the unavoidable frustrations children
experience when their needs are not met perfectly and instantly. These
frustrations accumulate as children begin to develop their independence.
Separating from mother, a necessary aspect of maturing, is painful and
adds to childrens' frustrations with their mothers. In this chapter, while
establishing a theoretical framework for a closer reading of the novels, I
will overview some dominant voices in the psychoanalytic mothering-
theory debate and analyze how these theories can shed light on Victorian
writers and works.

The Development of Mothering Theories

Mothering theories have grown out of transformations in Freudian concepts that occurred early in the development of psychoanalysis. Sigmund
Freud "knew little . . . about the infant's hostility toward the mother,"
and, in fact, focused instead on hostilities toward the father; according to
Reuben Fine in The History of Psychoanalysis, mother/child relations did
not become a dominant focus of study until 1940, a year after Freud's
death.[4] In tracing how Freud's theories have evolved throughout the twentieth century, John Bowlby in "Changing Theories of Childhood Since
Freud" discusses how drive theory has been dropped by most psychoanalysts in favor of a focus on the relationship between the young child
and his or her parents, particularly the mother.[5] Freud did little direct
work with children, which helps explain gaps in his analysis of mother/
child relationships, but Anna Freud and Melanie Klein worked to fill
these gaps. Melanie Klein, in particular, furthered the understanding of
infancy through close observation and analysis of young children. Reuben
Fine asserts that "full credit must go to Melanie Klein for being the first to
explore in detail this period of life [from birth to three years]."[6]

Klein theorized that the ego develops from the internalization of
the mother's breast, which "forms the core of the ego and vitally contributes to its growth." According to Klein:

the infant feels that he concretely internalizes the breast and the milk it gives. Also there is in his mind already some definite connection between the breast and other parts and aspects of the mother. . . . If this primal object, which is introjected, takes root in the ego with relative security, the basis for a satisfactory development is laid.[7]

Margaret Mahler, John Bowlby, D. W. Winnicott, and others have concurred with and furthered these ideas of an internalized good object based on the mother.

But Klein indicated that even when the mother has been internalized positively and the relationship between mother and baby is healthy, the child still invariably experiences rage due to its frustrations, and this rage is directed toward the mother.[8] The infant's fears contribute to its rage as "it becomes growingly aware that [the mother] has the power to grant or withhold the gratification of its needs."[9] In "Love, Guilt and Reparation" (1937), Melanie Klein explores where adult feelings of hostility toward mothers originate. Klein writes that "the baby's first object of love and hate—his mother—is both desired and hated with all the intensity and strength that is characteristic of the early urges of the baby."[10] The mother is the source of all comfort but also the source of all frustration. When she does not answer the child's cries immediately or misinterprets the situation and does not end the child's discomfort, "hatred and aggressive feelings are aroused and he becomes dominated by the impulses to destroy the very person who is the object of all his desires and who in his mind is linked up with everything he experiences—good and bad alike."[11] The infant's anger can lead to fantasies of biting and tearing the mother, and babies may actually think they have inflicted these injuries and then have fantasies of repairing their mothers.

Pip in Dickens's *Great Expectations* experiences in adulthood the conflicting drives to hurt and repair the mother; his feelings are directed toward two surrogate mother figures, his sister (Mrs. Joe) and Miss Havisham. As shall be discussed in greater detail in chapter 3, both women hurt him, and both die from violent incidents for which Pip feels at least partially guilty due to his latent anger toward them. Miss Havisham's burning and Mrs. Joe's beating seem to be the outcropping of Pip's justified hostility, although he is not directly responsible. Following Klein's model of hostility and then reparation, Pip makes reparation to both women in his care of them after they've been injured. The pattern of hostility and reparation appears in several of Dickens's novels and in his own troubled relations with his mother, as I shall show.

Melanie Klein argued that artistic creation often is motivated by a desire to make up for hostilities felt against the mother: "creativity stems," she asserted, "from the desire to make reparation to the mother for the injuries that the child has done to her psychologically."[12] In fact, Klein saw that achievement in general often was motivated by guilt about mothers and a need for reparation. Pip's narrative, then, can be seen as a reparation to two mothers for whom he had hostile feelings. And Dickens's many narratives can be interpreted in this light; they often attack negative mother figures, but their very existence, Klein would argue, might be inspired by Dickens's desire to compensate for his hostilities toward his mother.

Although anger toward mothers is not as overt in Thackeray, Brontë and Eliot, their creative outputs still can be seen as the outgrowth of a desire to compensate for or repair unfulfilling, insufficient relations with their mothers. By giving birth to characters and exercising complete authority over their lives, the authors become the missing mothers they searched for or replace the present mothers who are unsatisfactory. Their art mends, at least in part, the fractures caused by their frustrations and disappointments with their mothers by allowing them to give and mould lives, if only through narratives.

Thackeray's Rachel in *Henry Esmond,* truly one of the strangest mothers in fiction, experiences the hostility/reparation cycle that Klein attributes to most mothers. Rachel catches a disfiguring disease from the eponymous hero after she has treated him cruelly (out of jealousy) and betrayed his love. As was the case with Pip, Henry does not consciously inflict his punishment but the guilt he feels about it suggests that the suffering caused seemed to grow out of his angry thoughts. The reparation that Henry pays Rachel is lifelong devotion and eventually a marriage proposal: she gets to marry the boy she mothered. The marriage somewhat diffuses the mother/child tensions by legally removing Rachel from the role of mother to Henry. The portrayals of mothers in novels by George Eliot and Charlotte Brontë do not tend to reflect Klein's hostility/reparation pattern as clearly; instead they more often mirror aspects of mothering theory concerning absent mothers, which will be discussed in the next section and in chapters 4 and 6.

The initial frustrations of infants with their mothers inform later tensions as the children continue to develop. Melanie Klein shows that the initial frustrations of girl children with their mothers are exacerbated by the jealousy they develop against their mothers in rivalry for their fathers' affection. The frustrations of boy children become intensified, according to Nancy Chodorow and Carol Gilligan, when mothers initiate

or at least encourage the separation between themselves and sons to ensure normal gender development.[13] Both boys and girls develop complex
guilt feelings in relation to their mothers because of these early hostilities
and because, as Naomi Segal suggests in summarizing Shulamith
Firestone's *The Dialectic of Sex,* girls and boys both join "the ranks of their
mother's oppressors" as they grow up.[14] In a classic vicious circle, the
children's hostile feelings toward their mothers lead to guilt, which leads
to more hostile feelings.

Dorothy Dinnerstein, Nancy Chodorow, and Carol Gilligan have
done much to develop Klein's theories of mother/infant relations and to
analyze the effect of these relations on the adult psyche, particularly the
effect of the infant's initial hostilities toward the mother. Dinnerstein describes how infants initially experience a long period of complete dependence on the mother, who is uncontrollable and not always reliable;
therefore the infant begins life connecting feelings of vulnerability and
frustration with the mother.[15] It is because of these deeply rooted infantile feelings, Dinnerstein concludes, that both men and women fear female authority even as adults, for female authority is

> the earliest and profoundest prototype of absolute power. It
> emanates, at the outset, from a boundless, all-embracing pres-
> ence. We live by its grace while our lives are most fragile. . . . Its
> reign is total, all-pervasive, throughout our most vulnerable, our
> most fatefully impressionable, years. Power of this kind, con-
> centrated in one sex and exerted at the outset over both, is far
> too potent and dangerous a force to be allowed free sway in
> adult life. To contain it, to keep it under control and harness it to
> chosen purposes, is a vital need, a vital task, for every mother-
> raised human.[16]

Dinnerstein attributes the predominance of patriarchies to the fear of
female authority caused by mother-dominated childrearing. Male authority, Dinnerstein argues, comes to be seen as "a sanctuary from maternal
authority," which had such omnipotent control at the dawn of life.[17] She
suggests that if children's initial rage and disappointment were not experienced under such a predominantly female presence, the infantile rage
against female authority would be less severe and more easily conquered
in adulthood.[18]

Certainly Dickens in his writings seems motivated by the desire to
keep female authority in check: he characterizes authoritative women as
monsters of irascibility (Sally Brass in *The Old Curiosity Shop,* Mrs.
MacStinger in *Dombey and Son,* Miss Barbary in *Bleak House,* Mrs.

Clennam in *Little Dorrit,* and Miss Havisham and Mrs. Joe in *Great Expectations).* Often these women are punished by death, disfigurement, or loss. He depicts "good" women, for the most part, as those who are docile and rarely assert much authority even over themselves. Thackeray often reduces and punishes his authoritative women, too, even the docile maternal authority of Amelia Sedley in *Vanity Fair.* Becky Sharp gets her comeuppance, too, but manages to triumph in the end (only after she has relinquished all rights to her son, however). Thackeray's ambivalent feelings toward motherhood are revealed by this novel in which the good mother, Amelia, produces a bratty son, and the bad mother, Becky, produces a good son. In Thackeray it often seems the best thing a mother can do is abstain from mothering, yet he still devotes much high rhetoric to the adulation of the stereotypical ideal mother, even when she fails. He has a real love/ hate relationship with the Victorian maternal ideal throughout his narratives. George Eliot and Charlotte Brontë more often restrain maternal authority by removing it—their novels are marked by the absence of mothers. In their works the lack of a mother seems to be the sine qua non of adventure for the female protagonists. The mother must be removed (or quelled) for the narrative to begin. Charlotte Brontë's Jane Eyre, Caroline Helstone, Shirley Keeldar, and Lucy Snowe and George Eliot's Hetty Sorrel, Dorothea Brooke, Maggie Tulliver, Daniel Deronda, and Romola all experience the absence of mothers, while they also all share a longing for an intimacy that seems particularly sharp because of the lack of mother-love in their lives. The female protagonists in Brontë's and Eliot's works also tend to avoid becoming mothers, as shall be discussed in chapter 4 and chapter 6. Characters are often missing mothers in Dickens's novels, too, but his bitch mothers make such a strong presence that maternal absence is not as noticeable as in Eliot's and Brontë's works.

These hostile and ambivalent portrayals are probably, in part, a reaction to the overly sentimental depictions of mothers seen in sources such as those mentioned in chapter 1: periodical articles like Andrew Halliday's saccharine "Mothers," guidebooks for women like Sarah Ellis's *The Mothers of England,* or poetic pieces like Coventry Patmore's *The Angel in the House.* Victorians seemed to be split by the angel/bitch dichotomy, unable, in most cases, to deal with women—and mothers in particular— in any other way. The dichotomy is still going strong today. Ambiguity in a mother, a creature so intimate to us, is difficult to bear. But sentimentalizing the role does not help. According to D. W. Winnicott,

"Sentimentality is useless for parents, as it contains a denial of hate, and sentimentality in a mother is no good at all from the infant's point of view.

It seems to me doubtful whether a human child as he develops is capable of tolerating the full extent of his own hate in a sentimental environment. He needs hate to hate."[19]

The sentiment surrounding mothers in many print sources in the nineteenth century no doubt encouraged many to try to reflect the sentimental portrayals in their own lives. The extent of the sentiment and the angel/bitch view of women would have made dealing with natural feelings of frustration with mothers even more difficult.

In the same year that Dinnerstein's work appeared, Adrienne Rich published *Of Woman Born: Motherhood As Experience and Institution,* which makes similar arguments about the origins of hostilities toward mothers, while usefully promoting a metaphorical reading of many psychoanalytic concepts instead of the traditional literal interpretations. In summarizing works by Karen Horney, Clara Thompson, and Frieda Fromm-Reichmann, Rich argues that penis envy is not the literal desire of a girl to have a penis but a wish for the power held by those members of society who have penises. (Horney suggested that penis envy was countered by males' corresponding envy of motherhood, another source of their hostility toward women.)[20] Adding to the mothering-theory dialogue, Rich points out that an important reason for the resistance to mothers and women in general has been their connection with chthonic power—earthy, natural, cyclical forces that remind us of mess and death. This power seems counter to civilization and therefore inspires feelings of fear and hostility. Rich indicates that Freud felt that "civilization means identification, not with the mother but with the father."[21] She also suggests that hatred of the mother stems from a fear of "a deep underlying pull toward her, a dread that if one relaxes one's guard one will identify with her completely."[22] Like Dinnerstein, Rich concludes that only coparenting can diminish hostilities toward female authority and lead to a nonpatriarchal society.[23]

Mothering and Gender Identification

In *The Reproduction of Mothering: Psychoanalysis and the Sociology of Gender,* Nancy Chodorow furthers the analysis of mother-dominated childrearing. Chodorow argues, as I mentioned earlier, that boys are more frustrated by mothers than girls, because as gender identities begin to form, "sons tend to be experienced as differentiated from their mothers, and mothers push this differentiation."[24] Girls, although they certainly feel resentment and anger toward mothers, never feel as separated from them. Mothers tend to experience daughters as extensions of themselves, which results in girls developing a less rigid, isolated sense of identity and a "tendency . . . toward boundary confusion and a lack of sense of separateness from the world."[25] In particular, she focuses on how children raised predominantly by a mother develop patterns of thinking and behaving that perpetuate in the next generation the tendency of women to be the at-home nurturers and men to be more distant physically and emotionally. Boys, because they feel differentiated from their mothers, develop a sense of self in isolation and separation, and therefore they tend to behave more insularly as adults. Girls, having experienced a greater sense of connection and bonding to their mothers, tend to seek out other intimate relationships as adults and grow into the role of nurturers for their own children. This pattern might explain why Dickens and Thackeray more often reflect current stereotypes in their mother characterizations than Eliot and Brontë do; the stereotypes would be an understandable result of the more distanced perspective on mothering (and, in fact, on all relationships) that the male authors would have experienced.

Carol Gilligan explores similar territory in her study *In a Different Voice: Psychological Theory and Women's Development,* showing how girls' identities are often continuous with their mothers', while boys' identities must be established through separation. But Gilligan focuses less on hostilities toward mothers and more on how the differences between girls' and boys' relationships with their mothers lead to differences in moral thinking, with girls being more relational and subjective in making ethical decisions and boys being more objective and rule-oriented.[26] These gender differences can be seen in every novel mentioned in this study but are most apparent in the conflicts between male and female characters in Charlotte Brontë's *Shirley*. In fact, in some of its passages about differences between Robert's and Caroline's or Robert's and Shirley's thinking, *Shirley* seems to be the direct inspiration for Gilligan's study, as shall be shown in chapter 4. Chodorow's and Gilligan's theories help to explain why the male authors analyzed in this study demonstrate more overt hostilities toward mother characters while the female authors' resistance to mothers is more subtle and countered by their depiction of characters whose longing for a maternal bond motivates their actions.

Mothering, Neuroses, and Psychoses

The mothering theories I've outlined so far have dealt almost exclusively with the effects of typical mother/child relationships. The hostilities and guilt created are not the result of mothers or children with mental illnesses. Mother-monopolized parenting, according to the theories, produces such disturbances even among healthy individuals. So if typical mothers can cause such problems with healthy children, imagine the difficulties they can conjure up with unstable children. And if good mothers can be so bad, imagine how bad a bad mother can be. In the psychoanalytic writings on mothering, just about every mental disturbance conceivable is traced back to negative or inadequate mothering: depression, psychic masochism, narcissism, schizophrenia, just to name a few. Edmund Bergler explains psychic masochism as a "revenge against the mother," in which one provokes others, gets rejected, and then flaunts the rejection as a way of hurting the mother.[27] David Levy blames overprotective and overresponsive mothers for creating egocentric psychopaths who expect the world to cater to them as their mothers have.[28] Harry Sullivan attributes schizophrenia to mothers who are "hostile, punitive, malevolent, restrictive, antisexual, clinging and more concerned with [their] own welfare than with that of the child," while John Rosen has stated that "every schizophrenic he had seen had had a directly destructive mother."[29]

Clearly, in the view of psychoanalysts, the presence of mothers can have negative effects; their absence, however, can be even worse. John Bowlby has stated that the loss of the mother when the child is between six months and three or four years old " 'is an event of high pathogenic potential.' "[30] According to Bowlby, "protest, despair, and detachment" usually follow the loss of mother, and if the child cannot attach himself to a new object, "detachment from all human relationships" occurs.[31] In *Maternal Care and Mental Health* (1951), Bowlby argued that a close, affectionate relation to the mother or surrogate mother was essential for mental health. In fact in the absence of this relationship marasmus can occur, "the wasting away disease of young infants" caused by "some defect in the mother."[32] The mother, it seems, damns if she does and damns if she doesn't. Considering that mothers can have such a debilitating psychological impact, it is little wonder that Victorian novelists vacillated between hostile characterizations of mothers and a pronounced absence of mothers, with the insatiable longing for mother-love a deep undercurrent beneath the surface tensions of the narratives.

Mothering Theory and Queen Victoria

Since mothering theories suggest that as adults both men and women resist female authority because it reminds them of their infantile frustrations in being dominated by a mother, one has to wonder about the attitudes toward Queen Victoria, the maternal authority on the throne throughout most of the nineteenth century. But Victorians in general did not seem to resist the queen's authority; in fact she was one of the most powerful and popular queens in England's history. Queen Victoria may have helped to diffuse hostilities by being so socially conservative: she was stridently against women's rights, for instance, and wrote that she " 'is most anxious to enlist everyone who can speak or write to join in checking this mad wicked folly of Women's Rights, with all its attendant horrors, on which her poor, feeble sex is bent, forgetting every sense of womanly feeling and propriety.' "[33] Also her subservience to her husband Albert and her statements about male superiority probably helped mitigate her image as a dominator. As Linda Shires puts it,

> on the one hand, [Queen Victoria] is the most powerful woman in the world with an empire at her command. In this sense her position is revolutionary even though her government is stable. On the other hand, she is a domestic body, a woman who depends on her prime minister and her husband to advise and to rule because she believes that women should not hold such positions of power in government.[34]

But even if the queen hadn't mitigated her authority by her belief in female subservience to men, Victorians had no choice but to accept her authority; given the situation, hostilities would most likely be suppressed or expressed in other forms. The degree to which Victorian societal norms restricted women socially, professionally, and bodily (via corsets and heavy garments) could be in part an effect of the forced submission to the authority of a female sovereign. Nothing could be done about the queen's power; all other Victorian women, however, could be excessively restrained to compensate for the submission to one woman. The attacks on mothers and absent mothers in Victorian novels also might reflect the need to squelch female authority in areas where such restraint would be possible.

The impossible expectations of mothers created in Victorian England through guidebooks for women, periodical articles, poems and short stories about mothers, the image of Queen Victoria, and medical guidebooks led to mothers being more revered ideologically than they ever had been before. But in actuality these same high expectations, coupled with the hostilities and fears created by childrearing that was dominated almost exclusively by women, led to an atmosphere of extreme ambivalence toward mothers. Out of these tensions grew some of the most psychologically rich, intelligent, poignant, and passionate novels of the century: *Bleak House, Great Expectations, David Copperfield, Dombey and Son, Jane Eyre, Shirley, Villette, Vanity Fair, Pendennis, Henry Esmond, Adam Bede, Middlemarch,* and *Daniel Deronda,* novels in which mothers are punishing, punished, longed for, attacked, but always powerfully present even in their absence.[35]

Notes

1. Ann Phoenix and Anne Woollett, "Motherhood: Social Construction, Politics and Psychology," in *Motherhood: Meanings, Practices and Ideologies,* eds. Ann Phoenix, Anne Woollett, and Eva Lloyd (London: Sage, 1991), 21.

2. Shari Thurer, *The Myths of Motherhood: How Culture Reinvents the Good Mother* (Boston: Houghton Mifflin, 1994), 267.

3. Ibid., 287.

4. Reuben Fine, *The History of Psychoanalysis,* new expanded edition (New York: Continuum, 1990), 34.

5. John Bowlby, "Changing Theories of Childhood Since Freud," in *Freud in Exile: Psychoanalysis and its Vicissitudes,* eds. Edward Timms and Naomi Segal (New Haven, CT: Yale University Press, 1988), 230.

6. Fine, 34.

7. Ibid., 279-80.

8. Ibid., 152.

9. Melanie Klein, *Love, Guilt, and Reparation and Other Works 1921-1945,* introduction by R. E. Money-Kyrle (New York: The Free Press [Macmillan], 1975), 250n.

10. Ibid., 306.

11. Ibid.

12. Fine, 272.

13. Nancy Chodorow, *The Reproduction of Mothering: Psychoanalysis and The Sociology of Gender* (Berkeley: University of California Press, 1978), 110; Carol Gilligan, *In a Different Voice: Psychological Theory and Women's Development* (Cambridge, MA: Harvard University Press, 1982), 7-8.

14. Naomi Segal, "Freud and the Question of Women," in *Freud in Exile,* 248.

15. Dorothy Dinnerstein, *The Mermaid and the Minotaur: Sexual Arrangements and Human Malaise* (New York: Harper and Row, 1976), 28.

16. Ibid., 161.

17. Ibid., 176.

18. Ibid., 191. See also Isaac D. Balbus, "Disciplining Women: Michel Foucault and the Power of Feminist Discourse," in *After Foucault: Humanistic Knowledge, Postmodern Challenges* (New Brunswick, NJ: Rutgers University Press, 1988) 138-60, and Azizah Al-Hibri, "Reproduction, Mothering, and the Origins of Patriarchy," in *Mothering: Essays in Feminist Theory,* ed. Joyce Trebilcot (Totowa, NJ: Rowman & Allanheld, 1983), 83-88.

19. Quoted in Elsa First, "Mothering, Hate and Winnicott," in *Representations of Motherhood,* eds. Donna Bassin, Margaret Honey, and Meryle Mahrer Kaplan (New Haven: Yale University Press, 1994), 147-61.

20. Segal, 244.

21. Adrienne Rich, *Of Woman Born: Motherhood as Experience and Institution* (New York: W. W. Norton, 1986), 198.

22. Rich, 108-9, 188-89, 235.

23. Ibid., 211.

24. Chodorow, 110.

25. Ibid., 109-10.

26. Gilligan, 7-8, 16-18.

27. Fine, 162.

28. Ibid., 158.

29. Ibid., 152, 162-63.

30. Ibid., 433.

31. Ibid.

32. Ibìd., 160, 156.

33. Quoted in Richard D. Altick, *Victorian People and Ideas* (New York: W. W. Norton, 1973), 58.

34. Linda M. Shires, "Of Maenads, Mothers and Feminized Males: Victorian Readings of the French Revolution," in *Rewriting the Victorians: Theory, History and the Politics of Gender,* ed. Linda Shires (New York: Routledge, 1992), 154. Margaret Homans in "Victoria's Sovereign Obedience: Portraits of the Queen as Wife and Mother" makes a similar point about Victoria's marriage countering the threat she presented as a female authority. Homans argues that "for Victoria's monarchy to become and remain popular, the potential disadvantage of a woman on the throne—specifically, the fears of female rule that a queen regnant would inspire—had to turn into an advantage for the monarchy's middle-class imposture. This, Victoria's early marriage made possible." Homans continues, "It was possible for her subjects to read her marriage as no different from any other, as a form of privatization through which women were defined as the complements and subordinates of men" (in *Victo-*

rian *Literature and the Victorian Visual Imagination,* eds. Carol T. Christ and John O. Jordan [Berkeley: University of California Press, 1995], 173).

35. In addition to discussing the power of absent mothers in Victorian fiction, Sally Shuttleworth also mentions several Victorian novels in which a mother is longed for when, in fact, she is actually present (Brontë's *Shirley,* Dickens's *Bleak House,* and Eliot's *Daniel Deronda* are examples). See Sally Shuttleworth, "Demonic Mothers: Ideologies of Bourgeois Motherhood in the Mid-Victorian Era," in *Rewriting the Victorians,* 44.

Chapter 3

Making Mother Suffer, and Other Fun in Dickens

Dickens, the Mother Who Created
Him, and the Mothers He Created

Dickens beats, burns, scars, and strikes with paralysis and muteness numerous bitchy mothers and surrogate mothers in his novels. Miss Barbary in *Bleak House,* Mrs. Skewton in *Dombey and Son,* and Mrs. Clennam in *Little Dorrit* all collapse with strokes and sink into muteness, then death. In *Great Expectations* Mrs. Joe is beaten into idiocy and muteness and dies slowly while Miss Havisham is burnt, loses most of her powers of speech, then dies; Estella's real mother is scarred and then tamed by Jaggers. The frequency of such portrayals, along with the sparsity of positive mother figures, indicates that Dickens, like an Ancient Mariner of Mothering Woes, felt compelled to continually recreate the story of a mother's neglect or emotional abuse of a child and then to punish such mothers. The prevalence of benevolent father figures in the novels merely emphasizes the negative or absent mothers. Dickens's delight in making mothers suffer suggests his desire to wreak vengeance on his own mother, whose love for him failed to meet his needs; yet it also suggests a need to break free of the pull of mother, which could threaten his own identity and ability to create. As I have mentioned in chapter 2, Adrienne Rich suggests that matrophobia can be caused in part by a fear that one's self will be absorbed in the mother completely unless efforts are made to enforce a separation.[1] The rich inventiveness and energy Dickens devotes to making mothers suffer indicates that particularly powerful and complex passions informed his ideas of mothers.

Certainly Dickens's tendency to punish oppressive mothers reflects his feelings toward his own mother, Elizabeth Dickens. As has often been noted, he expressed resentment toward her in later life because she sent him to work in a blacking factory at the age of twelve when his father, John Dickens, was imprisoned for debt in the early months of 1824. What was truly unforgivable, in Dickens's eyes, was his mother's desire to send him back to the factory even after his father was released from the Marshalsea prison and had ended his son's ignominious employment. As Michael Slater points out, this betrayal was particularly painful as his mother had been the first to stir his intellectual curiosity when she taught him at home. All the promise of that intellectual awakening seemed to be sold out because of his mother's eagerness for the paltry money he could bring in.[2]

There has been controversy among critics about how much to weigh Dickens's anger against his mother. As Richard Currie points out, several critics have tried to minimize the importance of Dickens's hostility toward his mother, but Fred Kaplan's persuasive psychological reading of Dickens in his biography emphasizes the significance of this early rupture.[3] I do not want to reduce Dickens's characterizations to reactions against his mother; certainly his fictional creations are far more complex than that. Yet to suggest that his relations with his mother are unimportant or only of minimal importance would be naive.

The pain of Dickens's blacking factory experience was intensified by the contrast between his own position and that of his sister Fanny, who was a student at the Royal Academy of Music. While at night he lodged apart from his family in a dreary house run by a woman he later characterized in *Dombey and Son* as an "ogress" and by day pasted labels on blacking bottles, his sister was studying piano and winning prizes at the academy.[4] Watching her being congratulated by Princess Augusta at an awards ceremony, Dickens felt that he had lost all hope for greatness in his future. He later wrote, " 'I could not bear to think of myself—beyond the reach of all such honourable emulation and success. The tears ran down my face. I felt as if my heart were rent. I prayed, when I went to bed that night, to be lifted out of the humiliation and neglect in which I was. I never had suffered so much before.' "[5] Dickens blamed his mother more than his father for this humiliation, since his father had eventually rescued him from the factory while his mother tried to send him back.

Later in life Dickens's mother betrayed him again as he attempted to establish a respectable bourgeois demeanor. Her indecorous dressing and behavior disturbed him. "My mother," Dickens writes in a letter to Maria Winter, "has a strong objection to being considered in the least old, and usually appears here on Christmas Day in a juvenile cap which takes an immense time in the putting on."[6] Later, when his mother was in a senile decline, Dickens wrote that "the impossibility of getting her to understand what is the matter, combined with her desire to be got up in sables like a female Hamlet, illumines the dreary scene with a ghastly absurdity that is the chief relief I can find in it."[7] Like Dickens, she was excellent at mimicry and loved dancing, but Dickens disapproved of her performances, which apparently did not suit his ideal of motherhood.[8]

Dickens also was embarrassed by his mother's tendency to borrow money from him at frequent intervals. Upon visiting his mother toward the end of her life when she was lapsing into senility, Dickens was struck by how she had deteriorated, but in a letter wrote that "the instant she saw me, she plucked up a spirit and asked me for 'a pound.' "[9] Although he found humor in the situation, the scene would no doubt remind him of her former desire to make a profit from him no matter what the emotional expense. Her interest in him often seemed more mercenary than motherly, at least in his own judgment.

In Dickens's eyes, then, his mother never appreciated or loved him enough, disappointed him in his childhood and adulthood, and often embarrassed him. These may sound like the petulant complaints of an adolescent, but he certainly had cause for anger. Yet such overt conscious complaints fail to explain the harsh rhetoric of his autobiographical statement to John Forster—" 'I never afterwards forgot, I never shall forget, I never can forget, that my mother was warm for my being sent back [to the blacking factory].' "[10] As Gwen Watkins notes, Dickens did not blame his father nearly as much for his degrading stint in the factory, even though it was his father's insolvency that sent him there.[11] Nor can his conscious complaints against his mother satisfactorily explain the battalion of wretched mothers who frequent his fiction, from panderers like Mrs. Brown and Mrs. Skewton to pugilists like Mrs. Joe, Sally Brass, and Mrs. Squeers, and to the ice-mamas such as Miss Murdstone, Mrs. Pipchin, Miss Barbary, and Mrs. Clennam. Nor can his overt complaints against his mother sufficiently explain his cruelty to the mother of his children,

Catherine, and the strange demothering effect he had on the women who lived with him, which I will examine later. Elizabeth Dickens's behavior is too facile an explanation and does not merit the passion and extent of Dickens's response.

The psychoanalytic mothering theories discussed in chapter 2 help to explain Dickens's relations to the mother who created him and the mothers he created. Isaac Balbus in "Disciplining Women: Michel Foucault and the Power of Feminist Discourse" usefully summarizes theories of Dorothy Dinnerstein, Nancy Chodorow, and others that relate to Dickens's hostilities:

> in all cultures it is a woman—either the biological mother or mother-substitute—who is both the source of the satisfaction and the frustration of the imperious needs of the infant; she is at once the being with whom the child is initially indistinguishably identified and the one who enforces the (never more than partial) dissolution of this identification. Thus it is the mother who becomes the recipient of the unconscious hostility that accumulates in children of both sexes as the result of this inescapably painful separation. The mother who is loved is also necessarily the mother who is hated.[12]

Dickens's initial feelings of frustration and betrayal, directed against his mother, would then be exacerbated by her later betrayals—when she wanted to send him back to the blacking factory, when she embarrassed him by her juvenile dress and behavior, when she nagged him for money. His conscious complaints against his mother would be informed by the infantile frustrations, so his reactions to his mother's behavior would naturally be more excessive than the situation would seem to merit. And his resentment of his mother would broaden to hostilities toward female authority in general, according to Dinnerstein.[13]

Such frustrations with the mother are not entirely negative; as Nancy Chodorow points out, they are essential in the formation of identity. If children never were frustrated by their mothers' failures to meets their outrageous demands, they would never develop a sense of the difference between self and (m)other. Differentiation increases for boys as gender identification begins: while girls can form their sense of gender in relation to their mothers, boys must form theirs in opposition to their mothers, and mothers, according to Chodorow, must "push this differentiation."[14] The initial feelings of betrayal by the mother, then, would have been exacerbated for Dickens by the separation of becoming "properly" gender-oriented.

Some feminist Foucauldians, such as Jana Sawicki, criticize the "global" or totalizing tendencies of mothering theory while still finding in it a valid and useful, albeit partial, explanation of some mother/child relations.[15] It is in this spirit that I suggest mothering theory as a partial explanation of some tendencies in Dickens's relations to women. Every time his mother disappointed him, each failure to demonstrate absolute, selfless love, would be informed by the subconscious, infantile rage at his mother's inadequacy. David Holbrook, in *Charles Dickens and the Image of Woman,* states that Elizabeth Dickens must have been seriously deficient as a mother to produce such a strong response in Dickens, and similarly Gwen Watkins suggests that "it seems . . . very likely that Elizabeth Dickens was in fact always a poor mother."[16] But mothering theory, as I have previously indicated, suggests that deep resentments are a natural result of female-dominated childrearing; even the most responsive of mothers would arouse hostility. The climate of mother-worship in the nineteenth century would intensify these hostilities, for Dickens could not help but compare his mother to the ideal upheld all around him in periodicals (including his own), guidebooks, Queen Victoria, novels, and general social expectations. Against the angelic ideal, no mother, as I've indicated in chapter 1, stood much of a chance; Dickens's mother, with her eccentric manners in later life and her brusque dispatching of her son to the blacking factory, fell considerably short. The attractiveness of the infinitely patient, self-sacrificing, eternally devoted maternal ideal, and its prevalence in early and mid-Victorian culture, would have strengthened Dickens's bitterness toward his flawed mother.

Dickens's reactions to his mother's betrayals reverberate throughout the entire range of women he created, inter- and extra-textually. Mothering theorists suggest how far-reaching the negative effects of mother-dominated childrearing can be. In chapter 2 I outlined Dinnerstein's argument about how an infant's initial utter dependence on a woman creates for both men and women a fear of the will of women: "Female will is . . . the earliest and profoundest prototype of absolute power," Dinnerstein writes, and "we live by its grace while our lives are most fragile." That is why, Dinnerstein continues, it becomes a profound adult psychological need to control female will and power, for "power of this kind . . . is far too potent and dangerous a force to be allowed free sway in adult life."[17] Dinnerstein's conclusion that patriarchy is the result of mother-dominated childrearing (since both sexes as adults in general prefer male authority to the frighteningly pervasive, initial authority associated with women) may seem too essentialist as Dinnerstein presents it, yet it does offer insights into aspects of Victorian power structures. The extent of patriarchal domination in Victorian England, according to this theory, would reflect on one level the extent to which men had been excluded from (or avoided) childrearing, thereby making female power something against which to fight.

Certainly female power seems to disturb Dickens, driving him not only to punish powerful mother characters, but also to create a host of docile girl-women who haunt his pages—Rose Maylie, Little Nell, Ruth Pinch, Florence Dombey, Amy Dorrit, to name a few. These characters' self-effacement and devotion to family seem the embodiment of the ideals established in female guidebooks like those by Sarah Ellis or Mrs. Beeton and in periodicals like Dickens's own *Household Words,* which published Andrew Halliday's effusive homage to the martyrdom of motherhood (discussed in chapter 1). Significantly, none of these ideal, docile women characters are mothers in the main part of the narrative; all, except for Nell, are awarded motherhood in the last pages, but the depictions of them in these roles are so vague as to go almost unnoticed. Their achievement of motherhood compels the narrator to sketch the final tableau in a fog, then hastily pack up his materials and leave. With his selfless female characters, Dickens upholds Ellis's advice that a woman should "lay aside . . . her very *self*" and subsume her own desires in a life devoted to making others happy.[18] Dickens is not just reflecting and supporting the norms of behavior for Victorian women in such characterizations; he is recapitulating the psychological process that created such norms, that made the majority of Victorians (and, one might argue, even readers today) fearful of the will of women and desirous of keeping women restrained. Through his monstrous mothers he shows the fearful tyranny of women that leads him to prefer selfless women, women who must not venture into assertiveness, lest they begin to seem like mothers.[19]

Dickens's conscious resentments against his mother, coupled with more subterranean hostilities, led him to silence, maim, kill, or exclude mothers in every novel of his career. At least one protagonist in every single novel is missing a mother or loses one or more mother figures—harmful or not—in the course of the text. To paraphrase Lady Bracknell, to lose one parent is unfortunate, to lose more than one looks like carelessness. Or maliciousness. Granted, many protagonists are fatherless, too. But the strong presence of positive surrogate fathers makes up for the absence of biological fathers. Dickens creates positive surrogate mothers, too, such as Betsy Trotwood and Mrs. Boffin, neither of whom, significantly, are biological mothers, as Patricia Ingham notes.[20] But their numbers are sparse in comparison with the benevolent fathers: Pickwick, Wardle, Tony Weller, Newman Noggs, Gabriel Varden, Haredale, Sol Gills, Captain Cuttle, Toodle, Micawber, Daniel Peggotty, Jarndyce, Boythorn, Meagles, Doyce, Manette, Magwitch, the Aged P., Joe Gargery, Boffin, Wilfer, to name a few. By my count, benevolent fathers outnumber benevolent mothers at least two to one. And Dickens permits more of his friendly fathers to be biological parents, too, feeling, apparently, that biological fatherhood, because more distanced, is not as threatening as biological motherhood.

Mrs. Skewton in *Dombey and Son* and Miss Havisham in *Great Expectations* offer intriguing examples of Dickens reworking his hostilities toward his mother. Consider how in dress both mimic Elizabeth Dickens's habit of adorning herself absurdly and childishly. Elizabeth Dickens's "juvenile cap which takes an immense time in the putting on" sounds much like Mrs. Skewton's troublesome "peach-velvet bonnet," which, "perched on the back of her head, and the day being rather windy . . . was frantic to escape from Mrs. Skewton's company." The word "juvenile," which Dickens later used to describe his mother's cap, he applies to describe the rest of Mrs. Skewton's accoutrements: "diamonds, short sleeves, rouge, curls, teeth, and other juvenility all complete" (*D&S* 527-28). Mrs. Skewton's absurd accessories also call to mind the "sables" that Dickens's mother wore "like a female Hamlet." Also like Elizabeth Dickens, Mrs. Skewton cannot be made to understand the reality of her situation once she has had a stroke. She seems to think she can carry on the illusion of youth, but her attempts are embarrassing, even sickening. Both women are scorned, then, for trying to appear younger than they are, for resisting a stereotypical view of "mother," for humiliating their children.

Miss Havisham, surrogate mother to Estella and to Pip, takes such juvenile dressing to more horrific lengths, refusing to change out of the wedding gown she first put on as a young woman. Her attempts to freeze time are far more ghastly and destructive than Mrs. Skewton's or Elizabeth Dickens's: Miss Havisham's circle of decay and deception has a wider circumference. The similarities in dress between these two characters and Elizabeth Dickens are not the only connection, however. Both Mrs. Skewton and Miss Havisham repeat in varying forms one of Elizabeth Dickens's sins against her son. Mrs. Skewton basically sells her daughter in marriage to the highest bidder, just as Dickens felt sold to the blacking factory by his mother.[21] More complexly, just as Elizabeth Dickens had stimulated her son's interest in the intellect, in enlightenment and illumination, only to snatch that promise away and send him to the blacking factory, so does Miss Havisham seduce Pip with Estella, a star, a different sort of enlightenment, only to snatch her and the world she represents away and leave Pip in the dark. Both women are punished for their betrayals with painful, protracted deaths, Mrs. Skewton dying of a series of strokes detailed over 65 pages—five chapters—that render her increasingly senile, speechless, and hideous: "Paralysis was not to be deceived, had known her for the object of its errand, and had struck her at her glass, where she lay like a horrible doll that had tumbled down" (*D&S* 528). And later, "a dumb old woman lies upon the bed, and she is crooked and shrunk up, and half of her is dead" (*D&S* 584). Miss Havisham catches fire, "shrieking, with a whirl of fire blazing all about her, and soaring at least as many feet above her head as she was high" (*GE* 380). She thrashes around wildly as Pip tries to save her, then later falls into a stupor in which she can only say a few sentences, one of which could be considered a classic child's fantasy—the mother asking the child for forgiveness. Like Mrs. Skewton, she lingers for weeks (60 pages of text) in this half-alive state.

Miss Havisham's burning is preceded by a frightening vision Pip has as he is walking around the grounds of Satis House; in his mind he sees Miss Havisham hanging from a beam, and the vision so disconcerts him he returns to see that she is safe (*GE* 380). It is only when he goes back to her room and peers in that the spark ignites her dress. His vision seems at once a premonition and a vengeance fantasy, one that he both fears and desires. It is almost as if his own repressed anger and resentment for the pain she has caused him create the spark that sets her on fire. The flames reduce her to helplessness; Pip has her fate in his hands finally, just as she had his in hers, and he chooses to save her, at least from immediate death. The fire reverses their positions of power—the mother is contained and tamed; the son is scarred but victorious.

Mrs. Joe, another surrogate mother for Pip, also can be seen as a reworking of Dickens's hostilities toward his mother, since, like Elizabeth Dickens, she also seems willing to sell a young boy to the highest bidder in her eagerness to usher Pip off to Miss Havisham's. Of course her mistreatment of Pip takes more physical forms, too, in frequent beatings with the Tickler, a device that humorously but frighteningly captures the painful combination presented by Dickens's witch mothers: the name, Tickler, suggests a device for laughter and pleasure, while the actual experience of it provides only pain and fear. Dickens punishes Mrs. Joe with a brutal beating that renders her mute and idiotic, and she, like Miss Havisham and Mrs. Skewton, suffers a protracted death. As with

Miss Havisham's accident, Pip seems to be a distant agent in the punishment that Mrs. Joe receives. When he hears of the attack on his sister, Pip is "at first disposed to believe that *I* must have had some hand in the attack . . . or at all events that as her near relation, popularly known to be under obligations to her, I was a more legitimate object of suspicion than any one else." Soon after he finds that she was beaten with a convict's leg iron, and he is convinced it is the one he helped Magwitch to remove. "It was horrible," Pip writes, "to think that I had provided the weapon" that eventually takes Mrs. Joe's life (113-14). Pip's guilty feelings, his connection with the weapon, and the fact that his dark double, Orlick, is the actual attacker, suggest that at least on a subconscious level, he is guilty of a crime of vengeance on an irascible mother. The thought of getting back at his sister/mother for her cruelty would have to have been firmly rooted in Pip's psyche for him to feel such immediate and strong feelings of guilt.

Miss Barbary in *Bleak House* is another malicious mother struck down by Dickens with muteness and paralysis. The stroke that freezes her face and body seems a just retribution for the cold upbringing she has given Esther. She never shows Esther any affection, not even a smile, and concentrates on filling the child with a sense of shame, worthlessness, and duty that scars her more permanently than the smallpox she suffers from as an adult. As Patricia Eldredge points out, Miss Barbary wounds Esther with the worst message a child can hear—that she should never have been born.[22] Miss Barbary's death is not as drawn-out as Mrs. Skewton's or Miss Havisham's (she is, after all, not a major character, although definitely a major influence), but she does linger for a week in her stony state with her face "immovable" and her frown "unsoftened" (*BH* 19). (Dickens seems particularly fond of *silencing* his hurtful mother figures, as if their verbal assertiveness had been the worst sin against the docile maternal ideal. Along with Mrs. Skewton, Mrs. Joe, Miss Havisham, and Miss Barbary, Mrs. Clennam in *Little Dorrit* is also made mute.)

Having lost her real mother and having experienced a loveless relationship with a surrogate mother, Esther is motivated by a "desire for and fear of connection to mother," according to Marcia Goodman.[23] Goodman sees Esther's ambiguous feelings toward her mother as reflective of Dickens's own relationship to his mother. Using Nancy Chodorow's and Carol Gilligan's theories about the formation of gender identity, Goodman argues that through Esther, Dickens reveals his desire to return to the initial mother/son bonding experienced in infancy but also reveals his fear that such a merging would threaten his masculine identity. Males are more threatened by intimacy, according to Gilligan and Chodorow, because they must sever their initial intimate bond with their mother in order to pattern themselves after their fathers and establish a male identity. Goodman does not point out, however, that Dickens's conscious and unconscious hostile feelings toward his mother would make the impulse toward intimacy even more complicated. Goodman attributes Esther's difficulties in revealing her story—the hesitancies and coyness of her narrative—to her problems in reaching out for intimacy, problems that reflect Dickens's own troubles in this area.

Certainly complex emotions concerning mothers dominate *Bleak House,* with the narrative structured around Esther's move away from the influence of the bitchy surrogate mother, Miss Barbary, and toward the love of her real mother, Lady Dedlock, who cannot publicly acknowledge her. In between Dickens continues the focus on negative mothers through more minor characters like Mrs. Jellyby and Mrs. Pardiggle, both of whom neglect their children's needs in favor of their charitable work for natives in unpronounceable countries. These mothers are punished by domestic chaos, resentful children, and the collapse of the African philanthropic project, the one thing to which they had devoted time and attention. Caddy Jellyby, Mrs. Jellyby's neglected daughter, is a particularly poignant depiction of the sorrow caused by indifferent mothers. Her gloom and inability to assert herself directly result from a lack of maternal attention. The implicit message in Esther's and Caddy's upbringing is: if your own mother doesn't love you, nobody will, and therefore you had better not ask or expect anything of anyone.

Although Lady Dedlock cannot fairly be blamed for her inadequacies as a mother since she was led to believe her daughter was dead, Dickens still punishes her for not being there for her child by freezing her to death at the gate to the cemetery where her lover was buried. Her punishment parallels that of her sister, Miss Barbary, who was frozen in paralysis as punishment for being a cold mother. These mothers' deaths serve as both hook and closure to the narrative—one sets Esther's story in motion, and the other serves as the most dramatic climax of the plot after which the rest of the tale is denouement. Cold, inadequate mothers frozen in death stand guard at either end of *Bleak House* with indifferent mothers sprinkled throughout, suggesting that bad mothering and its consequences are the alpha and the omega of the bleakness of the world of this novel.[24] Esther, Dickens suggests, will reverse the bleakness by setting up a new world of her own, one in which she serves as the kind of selfless, loving, ideal mother that Sarah Ellis promoted in her guidebooks.

Dickens stabs at his own mother more directly (and more notoriously) through the character of Mrs. Nickleby, a garrulous, class-conscious, flirtatious widow who shows affection toward her two children but who seems oblivious to their needs and troubles, just as Dickens felt his mother had been oblivious to his. Dickens admitted that his mother was the model for Mrs. Nickleby, and one can see in his disapproving albeit comic portrayal of her loquaciousness and flirtatiousness a reflection of his disdain for these qualities in his own mother.[25] Mrs. Nickleby is not beaten, maimed, or killed as punishment for her failures as a mother, as are many mothers in Dickens. She is, however, restrained and silenced so that she can fit in comfortably in the respectable, bourgeois household that Nicholas finally establishes.[26] By the end of the text, Dickens reins in her garrulous monologues—which are one of the chief delights of the novel—and describes her as always maintaining a decorous demeanor and "preserving a great appearance of dignity" (*NN* 831). So she, too, is disciplined by Dickens, albeit more tamely.

The pattern of punishing negative or inadequate mothers continues in *David Copperfield* where Clara, David's sweet but ineffective mother, and Dora, David's sweet but ineffective wife, both die from a general decline following childbirth.[27] With these characterizations, Dickens does not so much vent hostilities toward his own mother; rather, he expresses the grief of a child and a husband at discovering the inadequacies of the woman with whom he is most intimate, the despair at finding her love will not meet his needs nor protect him from harm. These are the initial disappointments of the infant upon finding that his cries do not always elicit from his mother the perfect response, and they are the sobering realizations the twelve-year-old Dickens must have had when his mother seemed to harden her heart against his dreams of greatness and sent him off to the blacking factory. These feelings also are related to the disillusionment the adult Dickens eventually felt toward his wife, as shall be discussed later in this chapter. David Copperfield's mother initially betrays him when she brings the cruel Murdstone into their house as her new husband, thereby breaking the intimacy between son and mother. Then she fails to defend him against the tyranny and beatings of his stepfather or to prevent his being sent away. Her decline and eventual death after childbirth are punishments designed to fit her crime of inadequacy and weakness as a mother. She could not mother well, so her attempt to bring another helpless child into the world brings on her own death and the baby's.

As an adult, David chooses to marry Dora, a woman who, in her pretty girlishness and silliness, bears a resemblance to his mother. Dora's love fails him, just as his mother's did. It does not enable Dora to be a real helpmate to him; in spite of David's concentrated efforts to form her mind so that she might manage the house more practically, she resists the training, and seems, in fact, impervious to it. Her love for him does not produce the results he is looking for, and her punishment for this sin of omission is the same as Clara Copperfield's—she dies from a mysterious weakening following childbirth. As with Clara, Dora's death symbolizes her inability to be a mother, either to an infant or to the grown-child, David.

Like Pip and Esther, David gravitates from one inadequate mother figure toward another. Pip goes from his sister to Miss Havisham, Esther from Miss Barbary to Lady Dedlock, and David from his real mother to Dora. These novels are permeated with the longing and search for mother, for that initial feeling of union and harmony, that ultimate great expectation. The difference in Copperfield's case is that, unlike Pip and Esther, David eventually finds a good surrogate mother. In fact, he finds two, one in Betsy Trotwood and one in his second wife, the loving and nurturing Agnes. In *Bleak House* and *Great Expectations,* novels that come later in his career, Dickens is not as positive about the prospects of such a search.

Betsy Trotwood deserves a closer look as one of Dickens's most complete portraits of an ideal mother.[28] Reversing the mothering theory of child development in which an initial absolute harmony between the infant and mother is gradually and painfully broken, Betsy Trotwood *begins* by rejecting the infant David because he's a boy and later shoos him away when he arrives on her property, but finally she welcomes him, raising him with much love. Instead of starting out as a perfect source of comfort, only to end up a source of frustration, Betsy Trotwood inverts the pattern, with much more beneficial effects. She is Dickens's perfect mother, a woman with no biological children, living a compassionate but apparently sexless life alongside of Mr. Dick, raising a child in increasing instead of decreasing harmony and love. She is the kind of maternal authority Dickens can stomach—a loving, intelligent woman who still bows to the advice of the man of the house, even though he's an idiot. Mr. Dick's goofy lunacy would not, in most people, inspire confidence in his proclamations, yet when Betsy wants some "very sound advice" about what to do with David when he first arrives at her home, she turns to Mr. Dick for his opinion (which is: " 'wash him' ") (*DC* 193). Her ability to relinquish her authority to a man—particularly a man who acts like a little boy—redeems her from the tyrannous aspects of mothering. Her authority need not be feared because it is not complete and because she never fails David once she has accepted him in her home.

Other positive mother figures, like Mrs. Lirriper of "Mrs. Lirriper's Lodgings" and Mrs. Boffin of *Our Mutual Friend,* demonstrate similar dependability and affection, and, like Betsy Trotwood, they are not biological mothers. They are free, therefore, of the guilt all biological mothers share of breaking the initial perfect harmony between mother and child. Dickens seldom depicts positive biological mothers at any length; the chief exception to this pattern is *Our Mutual Friend's* Bella Wilfer, who becomes a mother entire chapters before the conclusion and is depicted in the role much more specifically than are Florence Dombey, Ruth Pinch, Amy Dorritt, or Esther Summerson. The portrayal is still far from realistic or fully developed, but it moves beyond the sketchy, last-minute pictures of heroines with children prattling around their knees that Dickens resorted to in numerous conclusions. It is interesting that Dickens's most positive biological mother does not appear until his last completed novel (begun in 1864) and only after his real mother died (in September 1863). Perhaps he needed to be released from her and partially purged of hostilities through many earlier negative mother characterizations before he could create a mother who is loving and dependable and who stays alive.

But Bella Wilfer does not mark the end of Dickens's fictional attacks on mothers. In "George Silverman's Explanation," originally published in *The Atlantic Monthly* in 1868, Dickens depicts the hero's mother as having "the gripe and clutch of poverty upon her face, upon her figure, and not least of all upon her voice" (*UT* 730). This drawn, bitchy mother has the habit of accusing her son of being " 'a worldly little devil' " (*UT* 730). Her constant accusations create in him a horror of becoming what she criticizes, and he consequently remains antisocial all his life. He ultimately contrives to have the woman he loves fall in love with his pupil, for his mother has blighted his life so severely that he feels it would be worldly of him to claim the young woman's love. His mother accuses him of worldliness even after he has given up his love, for she feels he must have gained some profit in it. This portrait of a cold mother, blind to her own son's good nature, seems as informed by Dickens's bitterness over his own mother's lack of appreciation of him as any characterization in his oeuvre. It shows that even in 1868, two years before his death, Dickens's resentment toward his mother could still well up as freshly as ever.

Dickens and Other Mothers

Dickens's hostilities toward mothers stray outside the confines of the page and his relationship with his own mother, however. Consider, for instance, his treatment of Catherine, the mother of his own children. Having born ten children in 14 years, Catherine was the epitome of Victorian motherhood. But, for Dickens, this image would have been ambivalent, at best. Any failure of Catherine's to meet his needs would have stirred up his adult, childhood, and infantile frustrations toward his mother. Nothing was as infuriating as the woman closest to him failing him. And Catherine did fail him. She became fat; her natural timidity and restraint in his eyes became slowness and dullness. After bearing ten children, she was no longer the light, blooming child-woman that he recreated recurrently in his fiction, that seemed to stir his fantasies so much. It was her fault, or so he needed to make himself believe, that he had to turn to Ellen Ternan for a more satisfying relationship. In other words, having become increasingly matronly and less girlish, Catherine became increasingly loathsome. And just as Dickens eliminated mothers in his fiction, so he did in his life. First he constructed a partition to separate his dressing room from their bedroom; then he had separation papers drawn up that essentially stripped Catherine of most of her children. Only her son Charley was to stay with her; all their other children stayed with Dickens. Dickens also felt compelled to rewrite Catherine's history, casting her as a bad mother. In the "Violated Letter," an explanation of his split with Catherine that Dickens wrote to Arthur Smith, and which later appeared in the *New York Tribune,* Dickens wrote that " 'the peculiarity of [Catherine's] character has thrown all the children on someone else.' " " 'I do not know,' " Dickens adds, " 'I cannot by any stretch of fancy imagine—what would have become of [the children] but for this aunt [Georgina], who has grown up with them, to whom they are devoted and who has sacrificed the best part of her youth and life to them.' "[29] The hyperbolic rhetoric of the passage, created mostly through parallelisms, reminds one of the rhetoric of his statement about his mother: " 'I never afterwards forgot, I never shall forget, I never can forget, that my mother was warm for my being sent back [to the blacking factory].' " But Catherine's own letters and the reports of her children and other family members contradict these accounts of her mothering.[30] Even Dickens's own letters from earlier in the marriage contradict his later reports. But once he had convinced himself that in some way she had disappointed and betrayed him, reason and memory appear to have been bent to serve the purpose of removing a bad mother from his and the children's presence.

Dickens had a strange demothering effect on other women who lived with him, too, almost as if they sensed they would lose the great man's esteem if they ever bore children. His sister-in-law, Mary, who helped Dickens and Catherine as they began their family, conveniently died just as she was entering marriageable and childbearing age. Georgina, the sister-in-law who took Mary's place in the Dickens household, never had children or married, turning down several marriage proposals. Dickens's eldest daughter, Mamie, also never married and devoted her life to promoting her father's reputation, while Dickens's only other surviving daughter, Katie, chose as a first husband an ailing, impotent man whom she seemed not to love. Naturally no children resulted from that union. And if Ellen Ternan ever had a child by Dickens, which we'll probably never know, she certainly never raised it nor made the mistake of becoming matronly in appearance.

In short, all the women to whom Dickens remained most devoted—Ellen, Georgina, Mary, his daughters—never became mothers in his lifetime, or were only mothers for a short time. The other women with whom he was close at various stages in his life—his mother, Catherine, his old girlfriend Maria Beadnell Winter—all were mothers and all suffered the jabs of his sarcasm, diminished devotion, even hostility. Dickens's esteem could not, it seems, survive motherhood.

With such pervasive antimother characterizations, passions, and actions, it is worth considering if there is more to Dickens's hostilities than his conscious resentments of his mother and the more infantile frustrations with her that psychoanalysis would suggest and that would have been exacerbated by unrealistic but pervasive nineteenth-century expectations of mothers. Was there something else about mothers that made Dickens punish and exclude them? For not only did he remove Catherine from his house, isolate her from their children, and rewrite her role as mother, but also he frequently contrived to flee the house around the times of his own children's births. He dashed off to the Garrick while Catherine labored with Mamie and the next day galloped off with Forster to go riding "for a good long spell."[31] During Katie's birth, Dickens was writing to Forster that he would "come to you directly I can leave home—may be in an hour, maybe in two, maybe in three . . . I shall drive down to you directly."[32] One gets the sense he was desperate to leave the house as soon as it was minimally decent to do so.

He continued the pattern with his other children's births. Two days before Walter was born, Dickens was frantic to leave the scene of impending birth: "Can you come to Hampstead," he wrote to Forster, "or to Greenwich—or to Windsor—or anywhere??????"[33] After Francis was born, Dickens wrote facetiously to Forster, "Nurses, wet and dry, apothecaries; mothers-in-law; babbies; with all the sweet (and chaste) delights of private life; these, my countrymen, are hard to leave. But you have called me forth, and I will come."[34] While Alfred was being born, Dickens went out to Gray's Inn Coffee House.[35] When Sydney was born, Dickens was unhabitually at home, but wrote to Macready saying he *wished* he could be in Birmingham where Macready was on an acting tour.[36] And when Dora was born in London, Dickens wrote to W. H. Wills saying, "Mrs. Dickens being happily confined, I go to Broadstairs this afternoon," as if there was some direct and obvious connection between Catherine giving birth and Dickens immediately leaving the scene.[37] The phrase "happily confined" takes on new meaning in light of his less-than-satisfactory relationship with Catherine. His wife is restricted to home, happily for him as now he can go away on his own. Finally, the week that Edward, the last child, was born, Dickens wrote a frantic appeal to Forster to plan a trip abroad with him.[38]

Of course, to put Dickens's behavior in a historical context, Victorian fathers did not hang around the birth scene as dotingly as some fathers do today. Still, I am not aware that it was exactly the custom to flee births with quite the determination Dickens did. But why? Did the messiness of mothers and births disturb his need for rigid, domestic order? As John Carey points out in *The Violent Effigy: A Study of Dickens' Imagination,* in Dickens's family life "his concern with neatness was obsessive. Each morning he went upstairs to inspect the drawers in his daughter's bedroom, and left notes reprimanding any untidiness."[39] He may have been drawn to mentally chaotic and eccentric characters, and the chaos of London streets may have invigorated him, but on the domestic front, he needed physical order, and that's not something easily come by in childbirth.

Perhaps Dickens also feared the earthy force represented by women in general and mothers in particular. As Adrienne Rich points out, the words for "mother" and "mud" are extremely close in many languages, which suggests a commonly perceived connection between the two.[40]

The great, natural, cyclical, and messy vitality that the childbearers of the world represent reminds us of both life and death, and therefore threatens.[41] Culture was created as an escape from such mortal cycles, an escape from earthiness, an escape from women. As Isaac Balbus puts it, "history has a meaning and that meaning is the flight from and the repudiation of the mother."[42] Camille Paglia, for once, concurs: we owe all culture, she claims, to men "repelled by [their] debt to a physical mother."[43] Perhaps Dickens sensed that his prolific output could only be sustained by keeping mothers at arm's length, as if he could get his pen stuck in their mucky vitality and never escape, never write, never be the great, esteemed man he knew he could and needed to be.

Whether or not Dickens was unconsciously "repelled by [his] debt to a physical mother," finally what is perhaps most fascinating about his desire to make mothers suffer and to exclude them is how much many readers *enjoy* the suffering with him. We experience a gratuitous glee in having Pip's sister pummeled, and a grim pleasure in watching Mrs. Clennam collapse, Miss Havisham burn, or Mrs. Skewton disintegrate. We cannot help but be fascinated by such suffering, while we, perhaps, vent some of our own infantile frustrations.

Dickens's need to make mother suffer, his impulse to reflect and support the norms of behavior established in guidebooks for women, and his compulsion to pick at his own emotional wounds may have warped his relations with women, but it also energized his wonderfully maddening and deliciously punished mothers. The longing for mother, the fear of her, and the anger at her betrayals propel his myriad of characters and his labyrinthian narratives. His yearning for the initial harmony of infant and mother motivated him to create recurrently idyllic conclusions replete with unions between friends, lovers, parents and children. Perhaps it is this yearning for the lost ideal mother that accounts for "the old unhappy loss or want of something" that haunts him throughout his life, a yearning without which he may never have been compelled to produce fictional worlds that recreate such losses and sometimes remedy them (*DC* 646).

Notes

1. Adrienne Rich, *Of Woman Born: Motherhood as Experience and Institution* (New York: W. W. Norton, 1986), 235.

2. Michael Slater, *Dickens and Women* (Stanford: Stanford University Press, 1983), 10.

3. Richard A. Currie, "Surviving Maternal Loss: Transitional Relatedness in Dickens's Esther Summerson," *Dickens Quarterly* 6.2 (1989): 62; and

Fred Kaplan, *Dickens: A Biography* (New York: William Morrow, 1988), 252.

4. Peter Ackroyd, *Dickens* (New York: HarperPerennial, 1992), 74-75, 86.

5. Quoted in Ackroyd, 86.

6. *Selected Letters of Charles Dickens,* ed. and arranged by David Paroissien (Boston: Twayne, 1985), 108.

7. *The Nonesuch Letters of Charles Dickens,* ed. Walter Dexter, vol. 3, *1858-1870* (Bloomsbury: The Nonesuch Press, 1938), 172.

8. Ackroyd, 7.

9. *The Nonesuch Letters,* vol. 3, 192-93.

10. Quoted in Edgar Johnson, *Charles Dickens: His Tragedy and Triumph,* vol. 1 (New York: Simon and Schuster, 1952), 44.

11. Gwen Watkins, *Dickens in Search of Himself: Recurrent Themes and Characters in the Work of Charles Dickens* (Totowa, NJ: Barnes & Noble, 1987), 19.

12. Isaac D. Balbus, "Disciplining Women: Michel Foucault and the Power of Feminist Discourse," in *After Foucault: Humanistic Knowledge, Postmodern Challenges* (New Brunswick, NJ: Rutgers University Press, 1988), 141.

13. Dorothy Dinnerstein, *The Mermaid and the Minotaur: Sexual Arrangements and Human Malaise* (New York: Harper and Row, 1976), 191.

14. Nancy Chodorow, *The Reproduction of Mothering: Psychoanalysis and the Sociology of Gender* (Berkeley: University of California Press, 1978), 110; Carol Gilligan, *In a Different Voice: Psychological Theory and Women's Development* (Cambridge, MA: Harvard University Press, 1982), 8.

15. Jana Sawicki, *Disciplining Foucault: Feminism, Power and the Body* (New York: Routledge, 1991), 65.

16. David Holbrook, *Charles Dickens and the Image of Woman* (New York: New York University Press, 1993), 173; Watkins, 23.

17. Dinnerstein, 161.

18. Sarah Ellis, *The Women of England; Their Social Duties and Domestic Habits* (New York: J. & H. G. Langley, 1843), 15.

19. Dickens's tendency to see mothers as all good or all bad can be seen as a symptom of what psychoanalysts call "splitting," a tendency that exists in most people but can be exaggerated in some. In one form of splitting, the child cannot assimilate the negative aspects of its mother into its sense of self or its sense of her and therefore "splits" them off. As Otto Kernberg has written (1975), " 'probably the best known manifestation of splitting is the division of external objects into "all good" ones and "all bad" ones, with the concomitant possibility of complete, abrupt shifts of an object from one extreme compartment to the other' " (quoted in Reuben Fine, *The History of Psychoanalysis,* new expanded edition [New York: Continuum, 1990], 310.) Although most people have a

tendency toward splitting, the tendency would likely be strong in Victorians because the predominance of the ideal-mother myth did not encourage realistic expectations of mothers.

20. Patricia Ingham, *Dickens, Women and Language* (Toronto: University of Toronto Press, 1992), 115.

21. Mrs. Brown, Mrs. Skewton's dirtier double, displays similarly destructive mothering tendencies, which lead to her daughter Alice's ruin. Mrs. Brown suffers her punishment when Alice returns and makes Mrs. Brown feel guilty for her bad mothering, treats her coldly, and then loses her looks (her mother's chief source of pride) as she dies slowly of a wasting disease.

22. Patricia Eldredge, "The Lost Self of Esther Summerson: A Horneyan Interpretation of *Bleak House*," in *Third Force Psychology and the Study of Literature*, ed. Bernard J. Paris (Toronto: Associated University Presses, 1986), 138.

23. Marcia Renee Goodman, " 'I'll Follow the Other': Tracing the (M)other in *Bleak House*," *Dickens Studies Annual* 19 (1990): 148.

24. John C. Ward has argued in "The Virtues of the Mothers: Powerful Women in *Bleak House*" (*Dickens Studies Newsletter* 14.2 [1983]: 38) that Esther and Lady Dedlock become stronger after they find one another. "The discovery of mother by daughter and daughter by mother has made both stronger, and more practically effective in opposing or overcoming the pressures of conventional masculine-dominated society," he states. The connection does seem to give them some emotional strength, but still Lady Dedlock ends her life in fleeing patriarchy—represented by her husband, the judgment of society, and the law—and in the last words of the text Esther is still the self-effacing female, avoiding saying anything too positive about herself. As Patricia Eldredge points out, Esther cannot conceive of trying to get out of her engagement with Jarndyce even though she is in love with Woodcourt, and in the end, it's Jarndyce who makes all the decisions for her. Eldredge sees this pattern as being the inescapable result of the absence of maternal love and her aunt's rejection of her in childhood (138-39, 151).

25. Ackroyd, 8.

26. Ingham, 83-84; Natalie McKnight, *Idiots, Madmen and Other Prisoners in Dickens* (New York: St. Martin's Press, 1993), 77-79.

27. It has been more common to see in David's courtship with Dora a reflection of Dickens's infatuation with Maria Beadnell (see, for instance, Edgar Johnson, *Charles Dickens: His Tragedy and Triumph*, vol. 2 [New York: Simon and Schuster, 1952], 687). But Peter Ackroyd writes that in David's romance with Dora "there are shades of Dickens's love for his mother and his sister, as if the novelist himself were looking back at the time of his own infancy" (588). Certainly there is affection in the portrayal of Dora, but there is also, undeniably, a focus on weaknesses and inadequacies similar to those Dickens complained of in his mother.

28. Clara Peggotty is another positive mother figure, providing David with much affection, support, and a second family with her brother, Daniel. Edgar Johnson (679-80) points out Peggotty's role as a second mother to David, but he does not note how she fails David in much the same way as his mother does. It is interesting that Dickens chose to give Peggotty the same first name as David's mother, for, like Clara Copperfield's, Clara Peggotty's love is inadequate in defending David against the Murdstones' cruelty and coldness. She, too, allows them to take over the house, abuse David, lock him up, and send him away.

29. Quoted in Slater, 373.

30. In *Dickens and Daughters,* Gladys Storey quotes Catherine's daughter Kate as saying " 'there was nothing wrong with my mother; she had her faults, of course, as we all have—but she was a sweet, kind, peace-loving woman, a lady—a lady born.' " Later when asked if a sister should ever live with a married sister's family, she said " 'Never, never, never—the greatest mistake; she (Georgina Hogarth) was useful to my mother, of course, but that was all. My poor, poor mother' " (New York: Haskell House, 1971), 22-23.

31. *The Letters of Charles Dickens,* Pilgrim Edition, vol. 1., ed. Madeline House et al. (Oxford: Clarendon Press, 1965), 384.

32. Ibid., 595.

33. *The Letters of Charles Dickens,* Pilgrim Edition, vol. 2, ed. Madeline House et al. (Oxford: Clarendon, Press, 1969), 205.

34. *The Letters of Charles Dickens,* Pilgrim Edition, vol. 4, ed. Kathleen Tillotson (Oxford: Clarendon Press, 1977), 20.

35. Ibid., 418.

36. *The Letters of Charles Dickens,* Pilgrim Edition, vol. 5, eds. Graham Storey and K. J. Fielding (Oxford: Clarendon Press, 1981), 58-59.

37. *The Letters of Charles Dickens,* Pilgrim Edition, vol. 6, eds. Graham Storey, Kathleen Tillotson, and Nina Burgis (Oxford: Clarendon Press, 1988), 58-59.

38. Ibid., 627.

39. John Carey, *The Violent Effigy: A Study of Dickens' Imagination* (Boston: Faber, 1973), 31.

40. Rich, 108.

41. Ibid., 108, 188-89.

42. Balbus, 142.

43. Camille Paglia, *Sexual Personae: Art and Decadence from Nefertiti to Emily Dickinson* (New York: Vintage, 1991), 9.

Chapter 4

Charlotte Brontë:
Moving from Mother to Mother

It is certainly not news that Charlotte Brontë's heroines are motherless, a condition they share in particular with Dickens's protagonists; many critics have mentioned this issue, but these analyses often fall short of appreciating the complex portrayals of surrogate mothers and attitudes toward mothering in Brontë's novels. The marked absence of biological mothers in Brontë coexists with a deep longing for maternal presence as well as a fear of succumbing to and even becoming a maternal authority.[1] In *Female Friendships and Communities: Charlotte Brontë, George Eliot, Elizabeth Gaskell,* Pauline Nestor points out that all of Brontë's novels are haunted by " 'mother-want,' " but she argues that ultimately in Brontë's fiction "the conjugal relationship . . . is validated ahead of the maternal." I would argue instead that the conjugal relationship becomes confused with and subsumed by the drive toward mother and mothering.[2]

Adrienne Rich has convincingly shown how various mother figures guide and shape Jane Eyre as she develops throughout the novel that bears her name, but Rich does not address the ambivalence Jane exhibits toward female authority and toward her own role of mother.[3] Brontë's mothers are, in fact, more complex, and less stereotypical and one-sided than those of most other Victorian novelists. Miss Temple, for instance, is a kind surrogate mother in *Jane Eyre,* but one who maintains a certain reserve about her—she is an object of veneration, as Jane points out in first describing her—a temple, as her name suggests, something sanctified but distant. Jane states that Miss Temple "had always something of serenity in her air, of state and mien, of refined propriety in her language, which precluded deviation into the ardent, the excited, the eager: something which chastened the pleasure of those who looked on her and listened to her, by a controlling sense of awe" (*JE* 63). She is not the type who can fill Jane's hunger for intimacy and love, nor can she do much to save Jane and the other girls from their suffering at Lowood, even though she is the superintendent. They still go hungry, and Miss Scatcherd still torments Helen Burns.

Mrs. Pryor in *Shirley* eventually becomes a loving mother to Caroline, but initially she had abandoned her daughter. Once she does reclaim her role as mother, however, she plays it with conviction. With this portrayal Brontë comes closest to the maternal ideal established in guidebooks by Sarah Ellis and company. Having revealed to Caroline that she is her mother, Mrs. Pryor takes a delight in serving her daughter, and Caroline, normally reticent in making any demands of anyone, enjoys making requests for her newfound mother to fill (*Sh* 409-17). The portrait seems to suggest, as Sarah Ellis or Sarah Lewis might, that it is the child's role to demand, the mother's to be fulfilled in filling these demands. The only other depiction in Brontë that rivals this one for capturing the Victorian ideal of motherhood is that of Frances in *The Professor* when Brontë describes her staring lovingly at her sleeping child:

> she bent above the pillow and hung over a child asleep; its slumber . . . was sound and calm; no tear wet its dark eyelashes; no fever heated its round cheek; no ill dream discomposed its budding features. Frances gazed, she did not smile, and yet the deepest delight filled, flushed her face; feeling, pleasurable, powerful, worked in her whole frame, which still was motionless. I saw, indeed, her heart heave, her lips were a little apart, her breathing grew somewhat hurried; the child smiled; then at last the mother smiled too, and said in low soliloquy, "God bless my little son!" (*Pr* 277-78)

This is a quintessentially sentimental Victorian tableau, of the kind in which Brontë rarely indulges. Caroline's relationship with her mother echoes elements of this passage, but otherwise Brontë evades the image of the two-dimensional Victorian ideal mother.

In *Shirley*, Mrs. Yorke, another complex mother, is depicted as a severe and sour matriarch but one devoted to her children and one whose pragmatic attitude toward parenting can seem refreshing in comparison with the impossible images of mothers portrayed in Victorian guidebooks. When Caroline states that " 'mothers love their children most dearly— almost better than they love themselves,' " Mrs. Yorke replies, " 'Fine talk! Very sentimental! There is the rough, practical part of life yet to come to you, young Miss!' " and then she goes on to ridicule Caroline for being overly sentimental and romantic in general (*Sh* 387). Although her attack is ruthless, Mrs. Yorke has a point. Caroline has no practical experience of mother-love, either in the giving or the getting of it, and her overly romantic nature is in part responsible for the decline she undergoes that almost kills her.

Madame Beck in *Villette* is another tyrannical matriarch, similar to Mrs. Yorke; she does not seem to be a bad mother, and even Lucy has a grudging respect for her strength. Yet she spies on Lucy, steals her correspondence, and tries her best to separate Lucy from her one source of joy, Paul Emanuel. Certainly she strays far from the maternal ideal when it comes to affection, yet her practicality is unquestionable. Brontë does not choose to depict her solely as a monster, even though she was based upon Madame Heger, who brought her great misery chiefly by being married to the man Brontë loved (M. Heger from the pensionnat in Brussels where Charlotte studied and taught). Like Madame Beck, Madame Heger worked assiduously to keep the young English woman from the older professor, and her plans succeeded.[4] Both mother-figures, the fictional Beck and the real-life Heger, cause great grief and loneliness; Charlotte's letters to M. Heger begging for some response from him reverberate even more painfully than Lucy Snowe's desperation for Paul.[5]

In these characterizations and others Brontë resists the ideals established by the guidebooks for mothers and presents women who in many cases transcend the angel/monster dichotomy that such ideals perpetuate. The ambiguity of Brontë's feelings about mothering stems in part from her own motherless upbringing, her burdensome mothering experiences, and the oppressive female authorities for whom she worked. The isolation and loneliness of Brontë's life on the edge of the bleak moors is legendary. Having lost her mother when she was five years old, and living with a father who was extremely stern and distant, Charlotte had a very lonely childhood. In later years she tried to recall her mother but the pictures were fragmentary at best. The one that Elizabeth Gaskell records in her biography of Brontë is not even a moment of intimacy between Charlotte and her mother but instead a memory of her mother playing with her brother Branwell.[6] So Charlotte was left without a mother and without many clear memories of one.

Psychoanalyst John Bowlby writes that the loss of the mother be-tween " 'six months and three or four or more years is an event of high pathogenic potential' " and that what is most necessary for the child is to attach to a new source of affection.[7] For Charlotte, there weren't many choices. An aunt came to stay with them, but she, like the father, Patrick Brontë, maintained her distance. According to Elizabeth Gaskell, the aunt spent most of her time in her bedroom, even at meals; Patrick Brontë dined alone, too.[8] The family socialized very little with neighbors, so the Brontë children turned to each other for emotional sustenance. But when Charlotte's oldest sisters, Maria and Elizabeth, died in 1825, Charlotte, at age nine, became the big sister and little mother of the family. That she took this responsibility seriously is evident in the many letters Gaskell quotes in her biography that reveal Charlotte's persistent (and justified) concern for the health of her sisters Anne and Emily and her brother Branwell. As Gaskell states, "Charlotte's deep thoughtful spirit appears to have felt almost painfully the tender responsibility which rested upon her with reference to her remaining sisters." Even though Charlotte was less than two years older than Emily, "Emily and Anne were simply com-panions and playmates, while Charlotte was motherly friend and guard-ian to both; and this loving assumption of duties beyond her years, made her feel considerably older than she really was."[9] She mothered her fa-ther as well, particularly when he lost his vision to cataracts. She would read to him and tell him stories to keep him entertained, which seems, by all accounts, to be more nurturing than she ever received.

It was Charlotte who insisted that Emily stay at home instead of seeking work as the others did because Emily faded when away from the moors. It was Charlotte who sought medical expertise when Emily began her decline, Charlotte who took Anne to the seaside and attended at her deathbed, Charlotte who turned down visits with friends to tend to her father, Charlotte who nursed their old housekeeper when she was sick. Charlotte's role as mother to her siblings ended bitterly when first Branwell, then Emily and Anne all died within a year (1848-49).

Brontë's maternal responsibilities extended beyond Haworth Par-sonage when, at the age of 19, she became governess at Roe Head, a girls' school that she herself had attended. Brontë never took too well to her various positions as governess or teacher. The actual task of instructing the young, of helping to raise them, was tedious and exhausting for her. Gaskell assesses Brontë's shortcomings as a teacher:

> neither she nor her sisters were naturally fond of children. The
> hieroglyphics of childhood were an unknown language to them,

for they had never been much with those younger than themselves. I am inclined to think, too, that they had not the happy
knack of imparting information, which seems to be a separate
gift from the faculty of acquiring it. . . . Consequently, teaching
very young children was anything but a 'delightful task' to the
three Brontë sisters.[10]

Later, even more bluntly, Gaskell states that since the Brontë children
had never known their mother and had had such an isolated, subdued
childhood they "were ignorant of the very nature of infancy. . . . Children
were to them the troublesome necessities of humanity."[11] Brontë's first
governess position in a private home was particularly difficult as she was
put in charge of, in her words, "a set of pampered, spoilt, turbulent children . . . [and] soon found that the constant demand on [her] stock of
animal spirits reduced them to the lowest state of exhaustion; at times I
felt—and, I suppose, seemed—depressed."[12] She disliked what she called
the " 'rude familiarity of children,' " and proclaimed " 'I *hate* and *abhor*
the very thoughts of governesship.' "[13]

   As if the children weren't bad enough, their mothers were worse.
In addition to her tense relations with Madame Heger, Brontë had strained
relations with at least one other woman for whom she worked, the mother
of the first children for whom she was a governess. Her first mistress
chastised her for not being more cheerful " 'with a sternness of manner
and a harshness of language scarcely credible.' "[14] Brontë describes the
woman as having no sympathy for her at all, and Charlotte was pained
by her lack of interest in communicating with her. The woman isolated
her, as Madame Heger did later. Madame Heger shunned Charlotte's society, according to Gaskell, because of religious differences—Heger was
Catholic and Charlotte was vehemently anti-Catholic—but biographers
Margot Peters, Winifred Gerin, and Alan Shelston indicate that Madame
Heger's chilliness was more directly motivated by her awareness of
Charlotte's infatuation with her husband.[15]

   Considering the extent of Brontë's responsibilities for her family
and her other charges, the early age at which she assumed such duties,
and the bitter experiences she had as a mother-figure and with mothers,
it is little wonder she pictures Jane Eyre as having nightmares about being "burdened with the charge of a little child . . . which shivered in my
cold arms and wailed piteously in my ear." In the dream, Rochester, the
person she really wants to be with, is "on the road a long way before
[her]" but the child holds her back (*JE* 247-48). The dream seems not
only to reflect the hindrances of Charlotte's life before and during the

writing of *Jane Eyre,* but it also seems to predict the burden and tragedy that marriage and pregnancy would be for her.[16] About six months after marrying Arthur Bell Nichols, Charlotte became very ill with constant nausea and faintness. She was suffering the combined effects of pregnancy and tuberculosis, according to Alan Shelston, but it is hard to ignore the likely psychological causes as well.[17] Her ambivalence to children in her life and art would have made thoughts of impending motherhood disturbing, even threatening; it doesn't take much imagination to see Brontë's extreme morning sickness as in part a rejection of both the fetus and the role of mother.[18]

Having been inside the mothering experience in numerous capacities, Brontë had a truer sense of its realities than did the male authors who were her contemporaries. Her experiences and observations about maternal relationships led to a progressive cynicism in her assessment of the possibility of establishing a complete bonding with another human being, the need for which is at the root of the longing for mother. In Brontë's novels, the longing for mother often takes the form of a desire for a perfect union reminiscent of the initial infant/mother bonding. The periods of crushing loneliness experienced by Jane Eyre, Lucy Snowe, and Caroline Helstone are fueled by their motherlessness; they keenly feel the need of someone to love them with the intensity, selflessness, and unconditionality of a mother. (Perhaps readers have identified with Brontë's heroines so closely over the last century and a half because the feeling of orphanhood is at one level universal. According to psychoanalytic mothering theories, all of us have suffered a severance from our mothers that frustrates and isolates us, all have felt abandoned by a mother to a degree). Brontë's heroines cannot find the perfect mother/child union, and even if they could, such a relationship would smack of regression and threaten identity. The longing for the union with mother is projected, then, onto a lover. Strange confusions between the roles of mother and lover reoccur in Brontë's novels. With a lover there is the hope of reestablishing the perfect physical and emotional merging of the initial infant/mother relationship. But a lover can threaten identity, too, so Brontë must chasten, wound, even kill the lovers to keep their power in check, as Adrienne Rich, Sandra Gilbert, and Susan Gubar have pointed out.[19] In the case of *Jane Eyre* and *Shirley* these attacks on the lovers allow Jane, Caroline, and Shirley to act as mothers to their lovers, to nurse them back to health, to provide for them. By becoming mothers to their lovers these female protagonists become the mothers that they sought, and, for a time, preserve their selves even within an intimate relationship. In *Villette,* the last novel of her career, Charlotte Brontë is less optimistic about the possibilities of such a solution; she brings about a momentary perfect union but it comes as part of a watery apocalypse that ends with a still-birth and no child/lover left to mother.

Becoming and Unbecoming Mother in *Jane Eyre*

Jane Eyre seems to be motivated by the desire to be mothered and to mother. She is propelled by a yearning for the love she has missed because she lost both parents when she was very young and had only a bitchy surrogate mother as a substitute. But she demonstrates ambivalence toward the roles of both loving mother and loved child. She is a prickly creature and needs to keep those she mothers and those who mother her at arms length in spite of the need that motivates her, for the mothering relationship is imbued for her with hostilities that stem from being abandoned, from experiencing negative mother-figures like Mrs. Reed and Miss Scatcherd, and from the fear of identity loss that can come with mother-love.

Jane Eyre opens with a tableau that poignantly captures Jane's isolation from mother-love. In this scene, Jane's cousins Eliza, John, and Georgiana are "clustered round their mamma," who, "with her darlings about her . . . looked perfectly happy," while Jane hides herself behind a curtain in a window seat because she has been banished from the cozy group by Mrs. Reed (*JE* 5). Mrs. Reed tells Jane that "she regretted to be under the necessity of keeping [Jane] at a distance; but that until she heard from Bessie and could discover by her own observation that [she] was endeavouring in good earnest to acquire a more sociable and child-like disposition . . . she really must exclude [her] from privileges intended only for contented, happy, little children" (5). Mrs. Reed is not the only mother-figure that Jane feels abandoned by in this scene; in her speech, Mrs. Reed distances the nurse, Bessie, from Jane as well. Bessie is the only woman in the young girl's life who ever shows her affection, and she does not dole it out in abundance, but by turning that erratic source of comfort for Jane into a kind of spy, Mrs. Reed furthers Jane's isolation. When Mrs. Reed locks Jane in the red-room for attacking John, the punishment is simply a physical manifestation of the emotional separation Jane has already undergone. She has already been locked away from the family. In the red-room, Jane fears that the ghost of Mr. Reed, who died in the room, will come back to avenge her—a favor she would prefer to do without—and when she sees a light on the wall she thinks it's his spirit and clamors to be let out. Mrs. Reed refuses to let her out even when Jane cries that she will be killed, and in an action emblematic of rejecting Jane's birth and very existence, Mrs. Reed thrusts the girl back into the red-room/womb and into a fit of unconsciousness. In this scene, the mother-figure temporarily but dramatically eradicates the unwanted child; the child momentarily ceases to exist.

When Jane finally is taken from the red-room, she awakens in the nursery and her deliverance is like a second birth, for she emerges with a defiant spirit that no longer expresses itself in animalistic fits but in precociously articulate words of protest. Her defiancé seems fueled by the injustice of being denied mother-love. In John Bowlby's work on the loss of mothers, he describes how most grievers go through stages of " 'protest, despair, and detachment' " in the grieving process. Bowlby states that if attachment to the lost object is not relinquished, " 'the end state is the most pathological of all—detachment from all human relationships.' "[20] Jane progresses through these stages in her grief for her lost parents and her rejection by her aunt. Jane oscillates between protest and despair and despair and detachment at Gateshead, but it is her protests, preternaturally articulate and impassioned, voiced against Mrs. Reed and born out of the red-room incident, that are most memorable:

> "You think I have no feelings, and that I can do without one bit of love or kindness; but I cannot live so; and you have no pity. I shall remember how you thrust me back—into the red-room, and locked me up there, to my dying day; though I was in agony, though I cried out, while suffocating with distress, 'Have mercy! Have mercy, aunt Reed!' And that punishment you made me suffer because your wicked boy struck me—knocked me down for nothing. I will tell anybody who asks me questions this exact tale. People think you a good woman, but you are bad; hard-hearted. *You* are deceitful." (31)

In this speech and others like it, Jane's protest rises above the occasion, to build an accretion of significance until it seems almost mythic. She scares Mrs. Reed with her words and her anger. Jane seems to be railing not only against a specific cruel treatment but against the fundamental injustice of having been brought into a world in which there is no steadfast source of love and fairness, no idyllic mother with whom she could live in harmony. Of course, even if her mother were alive, she would not have such a source, because such a perfect union is not possible, but she does not know that. Like children of all ages, she feels that unconditional love and fairness are her birthright, one she has been denied with the loss of her parents. In spite of her multiple griefs, Jane never sinks into what Bowlby considers the final stage of extreme mourning—complete detachment from others—because, as Rich points out, she always has at least one motherly presence nearby to keep her going: Bessie at Gateshead (who later names her daughter Jane), and then Helen Burns and Miss Temple at Lowood. These women help Jane to relinquish her emotional investment in what she has lost so she can bond with a new source of nurturing.

At Lowood Institute, Jane confronts another unjust, tyrannous female authority in the form of the sadistic Miss Scatcherd, whose flogging and reprimanding of Helen Burns seem to hurt Jane more than Helen. To escape the coldness and harshness of Miss Scatcherd and the institution in general, Jane gravitates to the kindness of Helen and Miss Temple, both of whom help to raise her and help her to learn how to master her temper, to be more of the angel and less of the fiend. Of course, their examples train Jane in the self-effacement that was the Victorian norm for women; they do not teach her how to harness her voice of protest. They serve as very traditional mothers, indoctrinating Jane with traditional values. It is indicative of Jane's ambivalence toward mothers—her simultaneous need for and fear of their love—that she chooses to ally herself with two women who cannot threaten her with too much intimacy, Helen because she is dying and Miss Temple because of her characteristic reserve. Jane longs for intimacy with mother at the same time she holds back from it. Maurianne Adams suggests that Jane's "drive to autonomy and an independent working life is undermined by her need for a sustaining and nurturing love," and the reverse also seems true: her need for love is undermined by her desire for autonomy.[21]

In the characterizations of Helen, Miss Temple, and Miss Scatcherd, Charlotte Brontë draws on her experiences at Cowan's Bridge School for clergymen's daughters: Helen is based on her older sister Maria, who died shortly after leaving the school, and Miss Temple and Miss Scatcherd had their counterparts in two of her teachers. These characterizations fall into the angel/bitch dichotomy more than any others in Brontë's work, perhaps because they stem from childhood, when passions are felt in their extremes and ambiguities go unperceived. The dichotomy pushes Jane forcefully toward Helen and Miss Temple as refuges. They are the temporary mothers she needs to continue to grow, to continue to be able to form attachments to other people. Helen and Miss Temple's love validates Jane's existence at Lowood—when they are both gone, Jane can no longer remain there.

Helen's death and Miss Temple's departure effect disruptions in the narrative that indicate just how much Jane depended upon them. When Helen dies, Jane ceases to relate a detailed account of her life, and, in fact, passes "a space of eight years almost in silence: a few lines only are necessary to keep up the links of connection" (72). In these "few lines" she tells of her successful studies and the role of teacher she has practiced enthusiastically for two years. She, too, then has become a mother-figure, helping to raise girls like herself, but it is interesting that she describes the role so sketchily. Why does she feel her achievement of this role deserves so little attention? Perhaps because it is dwarfed by the loss of another mother. When Miss Temple leaves upon getting married, Jane writes that "with her was gone every settled feeling, every association that had made Lowood in some degree a home." Miss Temple had been "mother, governess, and latterly, companion" to her; as is the case in many Victorian novels, the removal of the mother sets the heroine's adventures in motion (73).

As soon as Miss Temple is gone, Jane loses the feeling of serenity that had been part of her presence; her old self, the self of restlessness, protest, and passion, returns, and suddenly, in the space of a day, her old haunts are too confining. In an oft-quoted passage, Jane looks out to a hilly horizon and longs to venture out in the wider world. She makes a prayer first for liberty, then, feeling she should shoot for humbler goals, asks for change, and finally resolves upon "a new servitude" as the most she can request. The loss of another mother has left her groping for words to express her need and unsure what she has a right to ask for; the final choice she makes in her prayer is a phrase that suggests her desire to find another mother-type position, "a new servitude," out in what she calls the "real world" where there is "real knowledge" (74). Perhaps she wants a more "real" experience of mothering than what she has had at Lowood, something more intimate, more powerful, more all-encompassing.

The new servitude she finds is very much as a mother-figure—she becomes governess to the motherless Adele Varens at Thornfield. In her new position, she does not just teach the child; she raises her, since there is no one else on hand to do so. Rochester refers to Jane as Adele's "petite maman Anglaise" (216). Jane is pleased with her charge but not overly enthusiastic—she is inspired "with a degree of attachment sufficient to make us both content in each other's society" (95). Jane acknowledges the coolness of her attitude and further admits that this new servitude is not enough for her; once again she takes to scanning the horizon, wishing for a vaster range of experience and character. Having lost the stabilizing maternal presence of Miss Temple, Jane seems unable to cease searching for someone or something to fill the gap. She longs to be overwhelmed with experience, yet she resists losing herself in the role of mother to Adele.

The person who seems to answer her call, of course, is Rochester, who falls, literally, into Jane's life in response to her wish for more experience. Mothering plays a strange role in Jane's relationship with Rochester. Her simultaneous need to have a mother and to be a mother and her fear of losing identity in the very kind of intimacy she longs for affect them at every stage. Jane mothers Rochester at their first meeting when he and his horse have fallen on the icy road; she helps lift him, and helps him to walk by lending him her shoulder. This initial encounter somewhat mitigates his authority as an older man of a higher class so that the young, lower-class governess does not feel so powerless. Jane gets to reenact her role as protector to Rochester when she saves him from his burning bed, set on fire by his wife, Bertha. Rochester emerges from the near-disaster dripping wet and stunned, rather like a newborn child, and grateful to Jane for saving his life. Like a mother, she, in effect, has given him life, and he acknowledges his debt to her in what comes close to an avowal of passion. His warm words and looks raise Jane's hopes, so that once again, and not for the last time, her mothering of him when he is in need enables them to relate more as equals and thereby promotes their romance. His dependency on her is repeated when he calls on her in the middle of the night to help the wounded Mason.

After Rochester and Jane become engaged, however, Jane loses the position of nurturer, protector, and mother that had helped to advance their relationship. Suddenly, Rochester starts treating Jane as the child, calling her by endearments almost always accompanied by the word "little" ("my little wife," "little elf," "little English girl," etc.), trying to adorn her with jewels and fancy clothes as he would Adele. (It is interesting and prophetic that Jane addresses the visiting gypsy—actually Rochester in drag—as "mother," for this scene closely precedes her engagement to him when his mothering of her begins.) At one point Rochester compares his love for Jane to that of a man with "one little ewe lamb that was dear to him as a daughter" (262).

In spite of her yearning for love, Jane feels oppressed by Rochester's smothering attentions. She feels "smote and stunned" and fearful (227). She is too mature to play the role of child any more. Having visited and forgiven her dying aunt, Jane has come to terms with her past and buried (at least partially) the bitter, needy child she had been. The role of dependent does not appeal, and as Maurianne Adams states, Jane's hopes for herself and Rochester "are undermined by her conscious recognition of the disparity in their position and her inevitable reliance on him for everything."[22] She spends most of their engagement sparring with him and evading him as he gloats over his child, his toy, his "slave" (236).

Jane's increasing uneasiness at Rochester's treatment of her leads her, two nights before the wedding, to have nightmares of being burdened with a child. In one dream, as stated above, she is trying to catch up to Rochester on an unknown road but must carry the wailing child that prevents her from reaching him. In another dream, she stumbles through the ruins of Thornfield, still burdened with the child whom she cannot lay down anywhere. Gilbert and Adams both suggest that the child in the dream is emblematic of Jane's childhood self, the protesting, needy, angry girl that is still part of her and will be until she can unite with Rochester as equals.[23] Certainly the dream-child indicates how Rochester has resurrected and exacerbated those old feelings of being a burdensome child, but he also poses for Jane the implicit threat of *having* a burdensome child, of becoming a biological mother, not just a surrogate one for Adele, and the possibility frightens her. Although Jane has longed for that complete, harmonious union reminiscent of the mother/child relationship, she can't envision herself creating such a union, perhaps because of her own negative experiences with mothering and also the inherent frustrating contradictions of the role, which she finally confronts in the end when she does have a child.

The miserable dream-child permeates Jane's subconscious before the ill-fated wedding day; after, when the wedding and all of Jane's plans have been aborted, she gravitates once again toward mothers, this time the moon and a visionary mother, and then, as Adrienne Rich points out, to two mythic mothers, Mary and Diane. After telling Rochester that she must leave him, Jane falls asleep and dreams that she is back in the red-room where she had a fit as a child; once again she sees a light in the room. The ceiling dissolves into sky and the light seems to be the moon, but then it emerges from clouds, and it is "not a moon, but a white human form [shining] in the azure, inclining a glorious brow earthward." To her heart and spirit, the form warns, " 'My daughter, flee temptation!' " and Jane responds, " 'Mother, I will' " (281).

With this vision, Jane achieves the harmonious, perfect union with mother without sacrificing her identity. The vision demonstrates care for her without smothering her, without wiping out her independence as Rochester had begun to do. This vision gives Jane the strength she needs to leave, and she sets out on her own with "no relative but the universal mother, Nature" (284). This mother seems to Jane to be "benign and good; I thought she loved me, outcast as I was; and I, who from man could anticipate only mistrust, rejection, insult, clung to her with filial fondness" (285).

But Nature turns out not to be much of a nurturer, leaving Jane famished, weak, soaked, and cold; in this condition she stumbles onto Marsh End, the home of Diane and Mary Rivers, who, as Rich points out, "bear the names of the pagan and Christian aspects of the great Goddess—Diana or Artemis, the Virgin huntress, and Mary the Virgin Mother." Both, Rich continues, are "maternally tender and sensitive" to Jane, more nurturing than Mother Nature had been.[24] And, of course, they turn out to be Jane's cousins, which furthers the bond. But as close as they are to Jane in blood, intellect, and emotion, the mother/sister relation she has with them simply is not enough for Jane. She is haunted by concern for Rochester, and then quite literally haunted by his voice. " 'Jane! Jane! Jane!' " she hears him cry as St. John presses her to marry him and she asks heaven to reveal which path to choose (369). The moment is what Jane's whole life has tended toward—a mystical union with another human being—for in miraculously hearing Rochester's pained and urgent voice, her mind and his, her soul and his, are one, yet without loss of identity.

This mystical moment, in fact, seems to strengthen Jane's sense of self, for just at that moment she was going to sacrifice herself to St. John's missionary prospects, but instead she resists: "It was *my* time to assume ascendancy," she asserts. "*My* powers were in play, and in force. I told him to forbear question or remark; I desired him to leave me: I must, and would be alone. He obeyed at once" (370). This mystical experience parallels Jane's earlier vision of the celestial mother in white who warns her to flee temptation and her vision of the light in the red-room that brings about her new, strong voice. But now Rochester takes the place of the mother-figure that spoke to her, and the message is not to flee but to return to human passion.

As Rich, Gilbert, and others have pointed out, the Rochester that Jane returns to is no longer such a threat to her autonomy—deprived by a fire of his sight, a hand, and Thornfield, he is "symbolically castrated" and much more Jane's economic and physical equal.[25] He offers her now the perfect combination: he is both an older, parental figure who can no longer dominate and a person she can mother in an intense emotional and physical relationship. She can mother and be mothered. She still calls him master, but once again he must lean on her; she must be his second hand and eyes. " 'I love you better now,' " she proclaims, " 'when I can really be useful to you, than I did in your state of proud independence, when you disdained every part but that of the giver and protector' " (392).

Jane and Rochester's union brings to Jane other mothering opportunities that she does not relish quite as much. She visits Adele at her boarding school and, finding her unhappy, brings her home, intending to act as her governess. But she soon finds this plan "impracticable" because her time is so taken up with her husband, and so she sends Adele to another boarding school. Granted it is a closer and more indulgent one, and Jane clarifies that she takes pains to meet Adele's every need. But the haste with which Adele is dispatched in the conclusion and the lack of reflection in Jane's comment about the impracticality of keeping the child at home are telling.

Jane's relationship with her own biological child seems distant as well. She only mentions him once and not as *her* child but as Rochester's: "When his firstborn was put into his arms, he could see that the boy had inherited his own eyes, as they once were—large, brilliant, and black" (397). She does not say, "*my* child" or even "*our* child." Nor does she mention the son's name, yet she makes sure to state the names of the men Mary and Diane marry, seemingly much less significant characters.

Why the distance? With Rochester she can establish the perfect union she always has longed for, but with her own child she cannot. Part of her responsibility in being a biological mother is to help the child to become independent, to push the differentiation between mother and son. It's called raising a child. Having become the mother she longed for, she also becomes the initial source of frustration for her child. As a mother, she must initiate a separation that will set another tale of longing in motion.

Confusing Mothers and Lovers in *Shirley*

Jane Eyre concludes with an optimistic tableau of idyllic marriage—a perfect harmony of man and woman—and a slightly more troubled picture of mothering. In *Shirley* Brontë seems much less positive about the possibilities of either marriage or mothering, yet the yearning for mother dominates this novel as it did *Jane Eyre,* informing, once again, the relationships between lovers as well as those between parents and children.

Caroline Helstone seems scarred by the loss of her mother. Her loss is particularly difficult because her mother is still living, but her uncle tells her, with more than his usual insensitivity, that "wherever she is, she thinks nothing of you; she never inquires about you; I have reason to believe she does not wish to see you" (*Sh* 127). Such news is worse than a mother's death, for it rings of deliberate abandonment. By all rights Caroline should deeply resent her mother for leaving her, but instead she seems to take most of her anger out on herself in the form of low self-confidence, a lack of self-worth. As Gilbert and Gubar argue, Caroline's mother, Mrs. Pryor, "contributes to Caroline's passivity because she has withheld from her daughter the love that allows for a strong sense of self."[26]

Caroline's longing for her mother increases after Robert distances himself from her; in fact there seems to be a direct, inverse relationship between her longing for her mother and her intimacy with Robert—the more she has of the one, the less she has of the other. Her "deep, secret, anxious yearning to discover and know her mother strengthen[s] daily" when she is separated from Robert, "but with the desire [for her mother is] coupled a doubt, a dread—if she knew her, could she love her?" (201). The narrator explains that Caroline's doubts stem from the frosty manner in which others speak of her mother, but Caroline's apprehension about her ability to love her mother also suggests that some hostilities lurk not too far beneath the surface, although deep enough to be unconscious.

Caroline's motherlessness exacerbates her desperation when disappointed in love. According to the mythos of Victorian guidebooks and periodicals, her mother should have been a source of unconditional love and devotion. Instead Caroline was abandoned by her and, lacking any surrogate source of maternal love, Caroline does not have the strength to cope with Robert's rejection. As she tells Mrs. Pryor, "I wish somebody in the world loved me" (362). She contemplates this wish more specifically after Shirley has mused about mother Eve one warm summer night; on this occasion, Caroline's

> desire which many a night had kept her awake in her crib, and which fear of its fallacy had of late years almost extinguished, relit suddenly, and glowed warm in her heart: that her mother might come some happy day, and send for her to her presence—look upon her fondly with loving eyes, and say to her tenderly, in a sweet voice:—"Caroline, my child. I have a home for you: you shall live with me. All the love you have needed, and not tasted, from infancy, I have saved for you carefully. Come! It shall cherish you now." (316-17)

Like Jane Eyre when abandoned by Miss Temple, Caroline, rejected by mother and lover, wishes to become a governess, to seek out some larger world and some service in which she can at least nurture, if not be nurtured.

Right from the start, then, Caroline's longings for mother and lover are confused as her heartsickness over Robert's chilliness intensifies her yearning for her mother. Strangely enough, the connection between mother and lover is inherent in the relationship even before this time, however, since Robert is related to Caroline on her mother's side—her mother is the half-sister of Robert's father. Both her longings, therefore, share a familial aspect: Caroline yearns for closer bondings with both her mother and her mother's nephew. The two longings remain entangled throughout the entire novel.

One of the more intriguing instances of this confusion of mother and lover comes when Mrs. Pryor proposes that Caroline should come and live with her after Shirley marries so that Caroline won't feel she has to become a governess. At the time Mrs. Pryor makes the suggestion, Caroline does not yet know that she is her mother. Her offer mirrors Caroline's mother-fantasy, quoted earlier, but it sounds more like a marriage proposal than a mother talking to a daughter:

> "to you, my dear, I need not say I am attached; with you I am happier than I have ever been with any living thing. . . . Your society I should esteem a very dear privilege—an inestimable privilege, a comfort, a blessing. You shall come to me then, Caroline, do you refuse me? I hope you can love me?" (368)

Such might be the words Caroline would hope to hear from Robert, but instead they come from a woman whom she knows chiefly as the paid companion of her friend Shirley.

When Robert stays distant, Caroline sinks into a wasting illness that does not bring her lover to her but instead calls forth her mother from hiding. Even before Mrs. Pryor reveals herself to Caroline as her mother, she demonstrates her affection for the girl. She lets Caroline adjust her shawl and remove her bonnet and seems to be comforted by Caroline's touch, when she would have resisted the services of anyone else. Only in Caroline's presence does she really relax, and she takes more notice of Caroline's weakening condition than anyone else. It comes as little surprise to the reader, then, when Mrs. Pryor tells Caroline she is her mother. She does so because Caroline seems close to death and Mrs. Pryor senses that revealing their relationship and demonstrating her love will strengthen her. Of course, she is right. With mother-love at hand, Caroline turns a corner in her illness and begins to recover. Without it she could find no reason to live; with it she has at least one human being to bind her to life. "'If you *are* my mother,'" Caroline cries, "'the world is all changed to me. Surely I can live—I should like to recover—'" (410).

The world does indeed change for Caroline upon discovering her mother, for within moments of hearing Mrs. Pryor's declaration, Caroline transforms from being one of the most diffident, self-effacing characters in Brontë's works to being a fairly demanding daughter, ordering her mother to do several things at once, the last of which is "'take your supper here; don't leave me for one minute to-night'" (413). Mrs. Pryor seems a bit taken aback by her daughter's new, demanding approach: "'Oh, Caroline! it is well you are gentle. You will say to me go, and I shall go; come, and I shall come; do this, and I shall do it. . . . It will be always "mamma" prefacing a mandate: softly spoken though, from you'" (413). She even compares Caroline to James Helstone, Caroline's father, who was so cruel that mentioning him still makes her shudder.

Caroline justifies her imperiousness by claiming that it seems "'so natural, mamma, to ask you for this and that,'" but she does tell her mother to check her if she becomes too demanding. Mrs. Pryor asks her to check herself instead, for she lacks what she calls moral courage, by which she seems to mean the ability to stand up for herself, a weakness that she says is responsible for her having been an unnatural mother.

The mother/daughter tableau is revealing; Brontë suggests that no matter who plays the role of mother and child and no matter what their age, children will always be startlingly demanding of their mothers and mothers will always be at least a little stunned by the demands, even if the requests come from a newly found daughter close to death. Certainly Brontë depicts Mrs. Pryor as enjoying her service to Caroline: Caroline's "importunities were the mother's pleasure. If ever she delayed compliance, it was only to hear them repeated, and to enjoy her child's soft, half-playful, half-petulant urgency" (425). And Caroline enjoys her part, too: "'You will spoil me mamma. I always thought I should like to be spoiled, and I find it very sweet'" (425). But Mrs. Pryor's initial surprise at Caroline's demands and her comparison of Caroline to James Helstone reveal that even when Brontë was portraying a sentimental picture of a mother-and-child reunion, she did not let sentiment dominate.

Brontë almost never reflects uncritically the portrait that women's guidebooks presented of mothers; she remains conscious of the psychological tensions involved in the mother/child relationship, the burdens of mothering, and the dissatisfactions of being a child. The complete selflessness advocated by Sarah Ellis and company in their guidebooks for women did not strike Brontë as feasible or even beneficial. Caroline muses on the question of selflessness and concludes that "a terrible hollowness, mockery, want, craving [permeates] that existence which is given away to others. . . . Undue humility makes tyranny; weak concession creates selfishness" (190). Self-abnegation, in other words, often brings out the worst in others. Caroline should know, since her mother's concessions almost instantly make Caroline a tad selfish. (Her initial imperiousness is somewhat tempered, however, by her later expressions of delight in serving her mother and sewing dresses for her.)

Just as Jane Eyre can return to Rochester more as an equal after having established family connections, so Caroline can reunite with Robert after having discovered her mother. Having a mother, Caroline is less vulnerable, less desperate for his love—her existence no longer depends on his attention, and she is also, thanks to the presence of her mother, more practiced in asking for what she wants. But again as in *Jane Eyre,* the family is not the only factor that evens the score between the lovers— physical wounding and weakening help, too. In Caroline's case, Robert's gunshot wound not only debilitates him, it also keeps him in the kind of confining situation that frustrated her so deeply, and it enables her to mother him. His weakened, isolated condition leads him to be more open about his feelings for Caroline, and, in fact, in her first visit to him he is almost petulant with her for not having come sooner. They have shifted roles—she is in the position of bestowing or not bestowing affection, and she chooses to give it. She wishes she could give it uninterrupted by the interference of Mrs. Yorke and the nurse and says she would like him to be brought to the Rectory " 'and given to me and mamma,' " so that she and her mother could mother him together (542).

Caroline's confusion between Robert, her mother, and mothering continues as the novel closes. When Robert approaches Caroline in the garden to propose to her, she at first mistakes him for her mother. As she gazes out at the horizon, she feels an arm draw around her waist, and she responds:

> "I am looking at Venus, mamma: see, she is beautiful. . . ."
> The answer was a closer caress; and Caroline turned, and looked, not into Mrs. Pryor's matron face, but up at a dark manly visage. (593)

The touch of her lover and her mother are at first indistinguishable to her, and her desire for both seems equal, as she proclaims during the proposal that she could not leave her mother, not even for Robert (595).

Since Caroline's need and love for her mother has been inextricably bound up with her feelings for Robert, it is little wonder that the three agree to live together after the marriage.

Shirley also demonstrates a strong longing for a mother and a longing to mother that become entwined in her passion for Louis. Although like Caroline she has lost both parents, Shirley's desire is not as personal and immediate as Caroline's, perhaps because she has had the benefit of the companionship of Caroline's mother for years. She has a surrogate in Mrs. Pryor; what she craves seems to be a mother-goddess. She expresses her yearnings through mother-myths she composes. She waxes poetical about Mother Nature and compares her to Eve, the mother of all. The Eve she describes is a Titan:

> "the first woman's breast that heaved with life on this world yielded the daring which could contend with Omnipotence; the strength which could bear a thousand years of bondage,—the vitality which could feed that vulture death through uncounted ages,—the unexhausted life and uncorrupted excellence, sisters to immortality, which, after millenniums of crimes, struggles, and woes, could conceive and bring forth a Messiah." (315)

Shirley will not go into church because she prefers to stay out in Nature " 'with my mother Eve' " (316). The narrator contrasts Shirley's longing to be with her mythic mother with Caroline's longing for a more human maternal presence, one who would look at her lovingly and offer her a home.

Shirley explores the Eve myth again in a French composition she had written for Louis about a young orphan girl named Eva, who in the dawn of time was nurtured by Nature, which "nurses her, and becomes to her a mother" (456). Like both Shirley and Caroline, the girl wonders if any use is ever to be made of her intelligence and talent. She calls out for guidance, and it comes in the form of a *son* of God who calls her to him to reclaim " 'the lost atom of life' " that is her spirit. She returns to the heaven from which she came, and we're told that "such was the bridal-hour of Genius and Humanity" (459). The composition seems prophetic, for Eva deserts the comfort of Mother Nature for a male presence, just as Shirley deserts Mother Nature and her Titan-mother myths to yield to Louis. She succumbs to the gravitational pull of convention, abdicating the authority of her estate to a man instead of perpetuating her independence, developing her intimate sisterhood with Caroline, and striving to be a Titan.

Once again, however, the union between the lovers comes about only after the man has been physically weakened and the woman has at least tried to mother. Louis succumbs to a fever (which seems in part due to Shirley's relationship with Sir Philip Nunnely), and when Shirley visits his sickbed she is anxious to perform any little service that might aid him. Louis's pride leads him to refuse all her offers, but even still his weakness has temporarily shifted the power in their master-pupil relationship and dissipated Shirley's feigned aloofness.[27] Shirley's next attempt at nurturing him is more successful. When Louis hears that his brother has been wounded, he allows Shirley to comfort him and having felt her hand caress his he decides they must touch again, a decision that encourages him to act finally on his love for her (522). Their relationship is also advanced when she allows him to mother her when she has been bitten by what she fears is a rabid dog; she lets no one else in on her worries but Louis (476-77). In the end, Shirley again assumes something of a mother-role with Louis when he gets fired and she becomes his sole means of financial support. But, as I've suggested, Shirley chooses to relinquish her authority; for all her Titan-talk, romance depends on her being mastered.

Although Caroline and Shirley in numerous talks have enumerated the pitfalls of marriage, they both succumb to it, and Brontë depicts the results ambiguously. Intimacy has been established; the women get their men, tamed by their trials, but there is no idyllic picture here as there was at the end of *Jane Eyre*. Shirley pines for her lost liberty as soon as she has accepted Louis's proposal, and she drags her feet to the altar. The wedding bells seem to ring a death knell for both characters, for the narrator at the point of their marriages pulls far back from them, not giving us a word they spoke or a thought that went through their minds. The only report we get of their futures comes from the narrator's housekeeper, who only refers to how " 'bonnie' " the ladies looked when the foundation of the new mill was laid: " 'Mrs. Louis was the grandest, she always wore such handsome dresses; Mrs. Robert was quieter-like. Mrs. Louis smiled when she talked: she had a real happy, glad, good-natured look; but she had een that pierced a body through' " (599). We hear no report of any children produced from these marriages. The only issue of the marriage unions seems to be the "substantial stone and brick and ashes" of the Moore brothers' constructions. The Hollow, which was once "green, and lone, and wild" is now full of their buildings and business; Mother Nature has been mastered by the Moores, and so, it seems, have Caroline and Shirley, who after all their talk and yearning toward mothers and mothering, are left voiceless and apparently childless in the end.

Brontë does not portray an idyllic conclusion here as she did, in part, in *Jane Eyre* because she sees Shirley's and Caroline's longings for maternal presence paralleled in a great need and yearning for mothering in the community around them, a need often ignored or only partially filled. The workers, their wives and children, and the lonely and ridiculed spinsters all seem to need a more nurturing, compassionate environment. Caroline tries to tell Robert this early in the novel when she criticizes him for his heartlessness in dealing with the workers. And of course his hardness toward them directly leads to the riots and his wounding. She also tries to curb his ridicule of the ugly spinsters. Granted he does grow in compassion through the course of the narrative, but still his ultimate design for improving the lives of the workers is to ensure that he always stays successful so that he can continue to employ as many workers as possible. And, as suggested above, he has no compassion for Nature or those who love and live for her like Shirley, as he sets about realizing his plans.[28]

In many ways in this novel Brontë seems to be responding to Benjamin Disraeli's concept of the two nations, but instead of seeing the two as rich and poor, as he did in *Sybil,* she sees the two nations as men and women, or more accurately those who mother and those who do not mother. Prefiguring Carol Gilligan's theories in *In a Different Voice,* Brontë suggests that men are raised to fear intimacy and compassion as threats to their independence from mothers, challenges to their masculinity. But women, whose sense of femaleness is initially formed by bonding with a mother, seek out similar intimate bonds in other relationships.

These theories are born out in the novel. Robert goads his workers to violence not only because he purchases equipment that replaces them but also because he won't communicate with them—he maintains the distance between himself and them vehemently. He almost drives Caroline to her death because, again, distance is less threatening than intimacy. Caroline's desire to communicate and bond are characteristics he desperately needs, yet in Caroline these traits, unalloyed by a masculine sense of independence, almost destroy her. Caroline's mother saves her life, and the women's mothering of their lovers help to save their relationships. More of such mothering—involving nurturing, communication, and understanding—is needed to heal the larger community and to effect positive and permanent change in worker/factory owner relationships, but mothering gets marginalized in the industrial picture at the end, with Nature gone, the women silenced, and no children around. Brontë implies that the health not only of individuals and couples but

also of Nature and nations requires more intimate communication between men and women, more interchanging of ideas and roles, and more
power and influence for those who mother. But she also implies that
such conditions are not likely to occur.

Distant Mothering in *Villette*

Like her counterparts in *Jane Eyre* and *Shirley,* Lucy Snowe in *Villette*
suffers the loss of her mother (and, in fact her whole family), a loss that
sets her tale in motion. As with Jane, Caroline, and Shirley, Lucy's loss
fuels her drive toward establishing an intimate bond with someone else
and leads her to take several maternal positions. But Lucy seems more
scarred by her mourning than Brontë's other protagonists; because of her
grief and her naturally reticent personality (as well as circumstances beyond her control), she never successfully reattaches to anyone after her
family crisis. Psychoanalysts such as John Bowlby have pointed out, as
I've mentioned above, how essential it is for children mourning a lost
mother to reattach to another person after their initial despair. If such a
bonding does not occur soon afterward, a general detachment from all
people results. Lucy suffers from a modified version of this process; she
continues to be interested in others, even longs for companionship, yet
always remains strangely outside all her relationships, a voyeur to her
own loved ones. She secretly watches M. Emanuel and his coterie at the
festival (424-47), and unobserved she observes Paulina, her father, and
Graham in a palace park (396-97). While Madame Beck's surveillance
seems scheming and intrusive, Lucy presents hers as an inevitable aspect
of her being an outsider.

Lucy stays distant even in her own narration of the tragedies she
has experienced. As Gilbert and Gubar have pointed out, Lucy frequently
uses sea and storm imagery to describe catastrophes she has undergone,
without ever clarifying their specific nature, as if the losses devastate her
too much to be put in plain words—she must distance them even from
herself.[29] When she describes the tragedy that left her without a family,
she first tells the reader to picture her living happily for eight years, float-
ing along on calm waters. But then she admits that she must have fallen
overboard: "For many days and nights neither sun nor stars appeared;
we cast with our own hands the tackling out of the ship; a heavy tempest
lay on us; all hope that we should be saved was taken away. In fine, the
ship was lost, the crew perished" (28). She adds that even Mrs. Bretton
was not around to help her through her grief due to impediments that
again she does not specify. In short, in a page of very vague description,

Lucy chronicles the loss of two mother-figures and all other family ties. She returns to sea imagery to describe moments of disaster throughout the narrative, such as when she is left virtually alone over summer break and suffers a mental breakdown and again when M. Emanuel is lost at sea, as if all future ruptures resonate of the primal loss.

The turbulent, fluid images she uses to describe disasters are resonant of childbirth with all its water, blood, and tumult: "the rush and saltness of briny waves," "a heavy tempest lay on us" (28); "[suffering] seething from a bottomless and boundless sea" (143); and "it will rise— it will swell—it shrieks out long. . . . I cannot lull the blast" (450). The "oceanic" feeling, which psychoanalysts find at the root of religious and romantic ecstasies and which they attribute to a desire to return to the fetus's unity with its mother in the womb, strikes Lucy with horror. For her, oceanic feelings—feelings of being overwhelmed by a larger force— are portents of despair, dissolution, and grief. So her longing for intimacy, which demonstrates itself most forcefully in her relationship with M. Emanuel, also threatens her as it suggests the potential onslaught of oceanic feelings in which she would sustain even more losses.

In spite of her emotional distance from those around her, Lucy recurrently takes up the role of mother. She first mothers little Polly at Mrs. Bretton's house, but with no great show of affection. At first, without intervening, she watches the child cry herself to sleep at night and struggle to wash herself in the morning. She seems critical and disdainful of the child's excessive emotions and eccentric ways, calling her a "little busy-body" and "the little creature" (10, 16). Only when Polly is about to leave and is grieving over losing Graham does Lucy finally comfort her, holding her in her arms until she sleeps (27). But even in this intimate situation, with the young child sleeping in her arms, Lucy still seems emotionally distant: " 'a very unique child,' thought I as I viewed her sleeping countenance by the fitful moonlight" (27).

Lucy mothers Miss Marchmont with a similar distance and in her finds a warning of what life can be like if one withdraws from human affection. Lucy describes her as "irritable," "stern" and "exacting," and Lucy's heart sinks when she contemplates taking on the burden of caring for her. Their close living situation and Miss Marchmont's dependence on her bring about what Lucy calls "a sort of intimacy," but as in this phrase, Lucy always qualifies or subdues the positive remarks she makes about their relationship: "she could influence my sympathies (such as they were)"; Miss Marchmont displays "a character I could respect"; she "was rather like an irascible mother rating her daughter, than a harsh mistress lecturing a dependent" (30). Miss Marchmont claims that she was not always so morose. When she had the love of Frank, her fiancé, her heart was giving and glad; when he died, she shut up her heart. Before she dies she comes to regret her response to the calamity, and her tale should alert Lucy of how emotional distance can blight a life. But Lucy Snowe, aptly named, seems unable, by disposition and chance, to warm up. When Miss Marchmont dies, Lucy expresses no grief at all.

Lucy adopts new mothering positions in Villette first as care-giver to Madame Beck's children and then as teacher to the girls at the school. In neither role does she effuse about her charges and her duties involving them. She describes all the girls at the school as liars and finds them insolent, unruly, and unintelligent. Her critique of their characters keeps her at a distance from them even when she begins to enjoy her teaching. She likes teaching because it keeps her faculties sharp, not because she's thrilled at forming young minds.

Brontë's ambivalence is not just toward the mothering she must do, however, but also toward the mother in charge of her, Madame Beck. With this portrait, Brontë again reveals her ambivalence to female authority, seen also to a degree in Miss Marchmont and in earlier novels in Mrs. Yorke, Mrs. Reed, and Miss Scatcherd. Even Mrs. Bretton seems a chilly and at times insensitive, self-absorbed maternal figure. Lucy's discomfort with mothers slips out when she first encounters Madame Beck and, in describing her, equates the words "motherly" and "dumpy": Madame Beck is a "motherly, dumpy little woman, in a large shawl, a wrapping-gown, and a clean, trim night-cap" (55). Another interesting diction choice in the same chapter reveals a similar ambivalence. Lucy uses "pregnant" to describe a situation full of negative meaning for herself: "I saw quite well that they all [waiters and other servants], in a moment's calculation, estimated me at about the same fractional value. The fact seemed to me curious and pregnant" (50).

Mothering for Madame Beck is synonymous with spying and mastering—whether the subjects be her children or her teachers and students. She disciplines through surveillance, and, as mothering theorists suggest is the case with all female parents, she threatens the individuality and identity of those beneath her. Lucy's clothes, correspondence, companions, schedule, and livelihood are all at Madame Beck's disposal. Lucy is denied a self under the auspices of Madame Beck, just like a child with an overbearing mother.

The mothering that really breaks Lucy is her responsibility toward the cretin during summer vacation, an experience that she describes in a way that is reminiscent of taking care of an intractable young child:

> the hapless creature had been at times a heavy charge; I could not take her out beyond the garden, and I could not leave her a minute alone: for her poor mind, like her body, was warped: its propensity was to evil. A vague bent to mischief, an aimless malevolence, made constant vigilance indispensable. As she rarely spoke, and would sit for hours together moping and moving and distorting her features with indescribable grimaces, it was more like being prisoned with some strange tameless animal, than associating with a human being. Then there were personal attentions to be rendered which required the nerve of an hospital nurse; my resolution was so tried, it sometimes fell dead-sick. . . . Attendance on the cretin deprived me often of the power and inclination to swallow a meal. (141-42)

This mothering position demands all her energy and patience without providing any of the companionship, love, and stimulation she craves. Once the cretin has been taken away, Lucy abandons herself to her feverish exhaustion and walks restlessly, roaming past the city gates, goaded by "a want of companionship" (142). Mothering the cretin was bad; having no one to mother is even worse. Because of her lack of a stable, intimate source of maternal affection and her ambivalence toward mothering, which grows from her own loss and her negative experiences with female authority, being left alone to mother a subrational creature unnerves Lucy, and being left utterly alone unhinges her. She suffers a complete collapse. She flees to Mother church—the Catholic Church—for companionship and confession, but eventually it is her original surrogate mother, Mrs. Bretton, who restores her to health.

As was the case with Jane Eyre and Caroline Helstone, Lucy develops a romance in which mother and lover are confused. In Monsieur Emanuel Lucy finds a man she can mother who can also mother her. In her amused and affectionate patience with most of his tirades, she seems like an older, wiser, maternal presence in his life (308-315). Yet he also takes care of her, teaching her, proselytizing to her, and eventually supplying a home and school in which she can teach. Their union combines the roles of mother and lover effectively; they seem perfectly suited for each other.

But Brontë grew increasingly skeptical about such unions in her career as a writer. In *The Professor,* her first novel, the lovers marry and Brontë shows us an idyllic, sentimental picture of mother and son. In *Jane Eyre* the two lovers form a mystical unity in which they can hear each other's thoughts from miles away and a union they sustain years into marriage, but the issue of children is treated more distantly, as something that might interfere with the harmony of the lovers. In *Shirley* Brontë can't bring herself to show either idyllic marriage or parenting or even any resultant births, and she depicts the marriages as painful compromises for both women. Finally, in *Villette,* Brontë cannot bring herself even to depict a marriage, let alone children. She prefers to leave her heroine alone, independent, mothering only at a distance through her teaching. Granted Brontë does suggest a moment of mystical unity between Paul and Lucy when Lucy seems to know that Paul will drown at sea. At this crisis, Lucy's mind is at one with Paul's fate; in some ways, in fact, it seems as if she has brought about his shipwreck, as the images she uses to describe it are exactly those she has used throughout the novel to describe the other catastrophes she has experienced. Out of the sea-storm imagery that she has used to describe all her past disasters grows a real storm that drowns the lover coming to claim her as his bride, a lover whose presence would threaten her individuality, threaten her with the oceanic feelings of passion and motherhood.

In the ending of *Villette* it seems as if Lucy had read *Shirley* and taken to heart its overt and implied warnings about the compromises of marriage. The shipwreck seems an outward manifestation of her inner fears of intimacy, of having to mother full-time and permanently. Mother ocean swallows Paul instead of him swallowing Lucy, leaving Lucy to her teaching and her writing. It is through her writing that she can find fulfillment—make reparation with the mother, which Melanie Klein would suggest is at the root of all artistic creation—and create those moments of union that she, Jane, Caroline, and Shirley longed for but feared.

Perhaps Brontë should have taken the implied advice of her own novels and stayed away from what she came to see as the compromise of marriage and motherhood, for entrance into both proved the end of her. She writes optimistically about her marriage, yet between the lines the compromise she has made burns forth:

> "I really seem to have had scarcely a spare moment since that dim quiet June morning, when you, E-, and myself all walked

down to Haworth Church. Not that I have been wearied or oppressed; but the fact is, my time is not my own now; somebody else wants a good portion of it, and says, 'we must do so and so.' We *do* so and so, accordingly; and it generally seems the right thing."[30]

In a letter dated September 19, 1854, Brontë wrote of her married life that she had " 'not so much time for thinking: I am obliged to be more practical, for my dear Arthur is a very practical, as well as a very punctual and methodical man. . . . I believe it is not bad for me that his bent should be so wholly towards matters of life and active usefulness; so little inclined to the literary and contemplative.' "[31] Although she clearly admired her husband, she was feeling the constraints of married life, and in these letters one can hear her trying to convince herself that giving up her time and her own interests was justified in the name of marital harmony.

But Brontë's marital sacrifices make one uneasy as she seems to be giving up vital facets of her self. Just a few months after her marriage, she became pregnant, and the child who haunted Jane's dreams began to drag her into the grave.[32] Her pregnancy combined with her weak constitution and probable consumption killed her just nine months into marriage. Jane, Shirley, Caroline, and Lucy warned her, but her drive to establish an intimate bond won out.

Notes

1. Similar patterns can be seen in Anne and Emily Brontë's novels to a degree. In *Agnes Grey* the fear of motherhood is manifest in Agnes's nightmarish governess experiences with monstrous young charges; in *Wuthering Heights,* the fear of motherhood takes the form of deaths in childbirth.

2. Pauline Nestor, *Female Friendships and Communities: Charlotte Brontë, George Eliot, Elizabeth Gaskell* (Oxford: Clarendon Press, 1985), 104. Irene Tayler in *Holy Ghosts: The Male Muses of Emily and Charlotte Brontë* (New York: Columbia University Press, 1990) argues that both Charlotte and Emily Brontë longed for union with their lost mother. Emily envisioned such a union as unworldly and transcendent, but Charlotte, "who saw in her mother the model of woman as lovable and loved by the father, [and who] longed urgently to be lovable too," tried to reclaim her mother more in *this* world through her relationships and her art (7, 295).

3. Adrienne Rich, "Jane Eyre: The Temptations of a Motherless Woman," in *Critical Essays on Charlotte Brontë,* ed. Barbara Timm Gates (Boston: G. K. Hall, 1990), 142-55.

4. Margot Peters, *Unquiet Soul: A Biography of Charlotte Brontë* (New York: Doubleday, 1975), 128.

5. Peters, 149, 154, 159, 169, 170.

6. Elizabeth Gaskell, *The Life of Charlotte Brontë,* ed. Alan Shelston (New York: Penguin, 1985), 91.

7. Quoted in Reuben Fine, *The History of Psychoanalysis,* new expanded edition (New York: Continuum, 1990), 433.

8. Gaskell, 96.

9. Ibid., 111.

10. Ibid., 184.

11. Ibid., 210-11.

12. Quoted in Gaskell, 188.

13. Quoted in Ibid., 212, 195.

14. Quoted in Ibid., 188.

15. Ibid., 263; Peters, 128; Alan Shelston, ed. *The Life of Charlotte Brontë* by Elizabeth Gaskell (New York: Penguin, 1985), 590.

16. Peters, 406-7.

17. Shelston, 10.

18. In *Unquiet Soul,* Margot Peters indicates that the medical term for the sickness that led to Brontë's death is " 'hyperemesis gravidarum,' " which is basically acute and persistent morning sickness in pregnancy. Peters points out that "some doctors believe that hyperemesis gravidarum is caused by the mother's unconscious rejection of the baby" (410).

19. See Rich, Sandra M. Gilbert, "A Dialogue of Self and Soul: Plain Jane's Progress," and Susan Gubar, "The Genesis of Hunger, According to *Shirley,*" in *Critical Essays,* 154, 177, 248.

20. Quoted in Fine, 433.

21. Maurianne Adams, "*Jane Eyre*: Woman's Estate," in *Critical Essays,* 189.

22. Ibid., 181.

23. Sandra M. Gilbert, "A Dialogue of Self and Soul," 170; Adams, 192.

24. Rich, 152.

25. Rich, 154; Gilbert, "A Dialogue of Self and Soul," 176.

26. Sandra M. Gilbert and Susan Gubar, *The Madwoman in the Attic: The Woman Writer and the Nineteenth-Century Literary Imagination* (New Haven: Yale University Press, 1984), 392.

27. Arnold Shapiro sees pride as the chief barrier between Louis and Shirley and one of the two themes that bind together the private and public stories in the novel ("Public Themes and Private Lives: Social Criticism in *Shirley,*" in *Critical Essays,* 231).

28. As has often been pointed out, Brontë patterned Shirley after her sister Emily and in nothing is the similarity quite so clear as in Shirley's effusions about Nature (Gaskell, 379).

29. Gilbert and Gubar, 416-17.

30. Quoted in Gaskell, 520.

31. Quoted in Ibid., 521.

32. See Peters, 406-10.

Chapter 5

Thackeray's Oxymoronic Mothers

William Thackeray's mothers are, arguably, the strangest in Victorian fiction. He created mother-characters who are the epitome of the angelic Victorian ideal while at the same time being destructive, hysterical, even incestuous. Charles Dickens fathered forth angelic women who are seldom biological mothers in the main part of the narratives, and biological and surrogate mothers who are monsters, as I've discussed in chapter 3, but he never yoked the two together as radically as Thackeray frequently does in his fiction. In *Pendennis* we see the angelic Helen Pendennis pampering, smothering, falsely suspecting, and spying on her son until she drives him into a rage. The dutiful and devoted Amelia in *Vanity Fair* produces an overly proud, self-centered child, while the monstrous Becky turns out a decent, soft-hearted boy in spite of her inattention. In *Henry Esmond,* Rachel Esmond is a self-sacrificing mother who corrupts her role by falling in love with her foster son. Mrs. Prior in *Lovel the Widower* pushes one daughter into a disreputable career in the theater and steals shamelessly from her benefactors but all is done in the name of preserving her children.

All these mothers are a complex, disturbing mix—disturbing, in part, because it is difficult to tell if Thackeray is really in control of their contradictory natures or if at times he gets carried away by warring impulses in his own attitudes toward mothers, producing characters who reveal his own unresolved ambivalent feelings. In portraying maternal figures, Thackeray often seems driven to reproduce the stereotypical angel mother who held enormous attraction for him (and many others), but his satirical side could not be repressed for very long and inevitably found the cracks in the image. "Mockery lies coiled within [the] praise" of such angels as Amelia Sedley.[1] Emotionally he cherishes the dream of the perfect mother, while intellectually he scorns both the belief in such perfection and the attempt to achieve it. The tensions between his longing for the stereotypical angel-mother and his love of satire charge his female parents with a strange, unstable energy.

Another distinguishing feature of Thackeray's mothers is the amount of time he devotes to them in his novels. Dickens in most cases retreats from his narratives once the heroines become mothers, leaving only a foggy picture of their parental lives in the end. Charlotte Brontë does the same in *Jane Eyre* and avoids motherhood with the heroines of her next two novels. George Eliot similarly avoids or distances the picture of her heroines as mothers, except for Hetty Sorrel, who distinguishes herself as a mother by the extremes she goes to in order to avoid mothering. But Thackeray in his first novel gives us almost half the book to witness Amelia and Becky as parents. In *Pendennis,* Arthur's mother dominates the narrative far more than any of the younger women he courts. In *Henry Esmond* the narrative develops Rachel's character even more vividly than Henry's, as she evolves from Henry's foster-mother to his wife. And in *Lovel the Widower,* although the chief interest stems from the humorous, self-deprecating, and caustic narrative voice, the machinations of mothers and mothers-in-law take a close second.

Thackeray's Missing Mothers

Perhaps Thackeray devoted more novel-space to mothers than most other major Victorian writers did because such characters were notably absent in his own life. He filled in with words what he'd missed in the flesh for much of his childhood and adulthood. He was separated from his mother when he was five years old and sent from his native India to a hostile school in England, about which he later commented " 'What a dreadful place that private school was . . . cold, chilblains, bad dinners, not enough victuals and caning awful!' "[2] In *The Roundabout Papers* Thackeray writes that he used to go to bed every night praying he would dream of his mother.[3] As Gordon Ray points out, this early hardship probably was more devastating than Dickens's painful blacking-factory experience because Thackeray was only five at the time and much more vulnerable than Dickens, who was 12 when he faced his crisis. And Dickens at least had his family in the same city, whereas Thackeray's family was thousands of miles away in India. This early severance from his mother would have exacerbated what Nancy Chodorow has described as the child's early experience of rejection by the mother and frustration with her. Sons, according to Chodorow, feel even more separated from the mother than daughters do, and mothers tend to "push this differentiation" in order to encourage traditional masculine characteristics.[4] As a child, Thackeray seems to have repressed his frustrations with his mother and considered her an angel, as his later letters suggest, but as an adult the frustrations emerged, creating a much tenser relationship with her, which can be seen in letters and the ambivalent angel-women characters he patterned after her in his novels.

When his mother returned from India with her second husband, Major Carmichael-Smyth, nine-year-old Thackeray's affection for her both pleased and overwhelmed her. According to Mrs. Carmichael-Smyth, " 'He could not speak but kissed me & looked at me again & again, I could almost have said "Lord now let thou thy servant depart in peace for mine eyes have seen thy salvation." ' "[5] Years later (March 1848) when he was visiting his family's former home in Addiscombe, Thackeray wrote in his diary that "All sorts of recollections of my youth came back to me: dark and sad and painful with my dear good mother as a gentle angel interposing between me and misery."[6] Ray concludes that this mother/child relationship led Thackeray "to see life permanently in terms of a dichotomy between the warmth and trust of a happy home circle and the brutality or indifference of the outside world," which would in part explain the division between the sentimental and the satiric voice in Thackeray. But Ray adds that Thackeray's "remembrance of what his mother had been to him when he was a boy created in him a permanent need for the companionship of a woman whom he could love and in whom he could confide."[7]

Perhaps it would be more accurate to say that Thackeray's remembrance of what he had *wanted* his mother to be created his need for an intimate, maternal relationship, as she was certainly more absent than present in his early life. Even after the four-year separation when she was in India, Thackeray still lived at school most of the year, returning only for summer vacations at home. The geographic separations were most likely easier to bear, however, than her remarriage. As John Carey notes, Thackeray felt that her second marriage sullied her, and "it disgusted him to hear Carmichael-Smyth 'snoring in my mother's room.' "[8] When he recognized her old bed upon revisiting Addiscombe, he wrote in his diary that it made him feel "very queer."[9] Ray downplays such Oedipal tensions, yet they would no doubt be strong in a son as passionately devoted as Thackeray was to his mother. These tensions would have exacerbated any resentment he felt against his mother for sending him away to school at such a young age and for failing to meet his most basic emotional need—her presence—for four years of his life. His need for upholding the ideal image of her, however, kept him repressing his frustrations, which he did not seem to confront until they emerged later in fictional form.

Absence characterized Thackeray's relationship with his wife as well. During his courtship with Isabella Shawe, the girl's mother took a dislike to him and eventually moved to new lodgings and prohibited communications between the lovers. The severance seemed only to heighten their feelings for each other, however, and they managed to write to each other surreptitiously and married a month later. The first two years of their marriage were happy, but after the death of their second daughter, Isabella grew increasingly depressed, and Thackeray began seeking company away from home more frequently.

His wife was initially very much his domestic ideal; she after all was the chief model for Amelia Sedley.[10] But like Amelia she had few intellectual interests and could not share with Thackeray many of his literary and artistic enjoyments. She was like a child to him, a fact he vividly captured in a caricature he drew of the two of them walking down the street; he drew Isabella as half his height, about the size of a six-year-old child.[11]

Isabella's depression increased after the birth of their third daughter, but Thackeray was consumed with his work and growing success and did not heed her pleas to stay at home when he was asked to go to Belgium to write travel articles for *Blackwood's Magazine*. When he returned, his wife was much worse and a seaside visit did nothing to restore her. He took her to Cork to visit her mother and sister, and on the way she tried to kill herself by jumping overboard. The visit with her mother helped no one, and while their subsequent stay in Paris with his mother consoled Thackeray, it did nothing to improve Isabella's mental health. He sought treatments for her in France, Germany, and England but none helped, and he committed her to Esquirol's Maison de Santé at Ivry. He tried living with her again after her treatment at Esquirol's but her condition worsened, and he left her in charge of a Dr. Puzin for the next few years, after which he took her to England, where she was cared for by Mrs. Bakewell at Camberwell. They never lived together again.

Thackeray's mother ultimately served as the mother of his children; in other words, she took, in part, the role of his wife (we'll see later in this chapter that a similar pattern emerges in his novels where more than once a mother takes on the role of a son's wife). But he was separated even from his mother and daughters as he needed to stay in England while they still lived in Paris. In June 1845, he wrote to his mother complaining of his loneliness after she and his daughters had visited:

> I wish you had never come that's the truth—for I fancied myself perfectly happy until then—now I see the difference: and what a deal of the best sort of happiness it is God's will that I should lose. . . . the paper gets dim before my eyes and it is the scene of parting over again. . . . I never could bear to think of children parted from their parents somehow without a tendency to blubbering: and am as weak to this day upon the point, as I used to be at school.[12]

Absence from his mother and from the mother of his children—it seems that mothers dominate his narratives in inverse proportion to their absence in his life.

The other woman whose absence he had to endure was Jane Brookfield, the wife of a former college friend, William Brookfield. In a letter to his mother dated March 6, 1846, he writes of Mrs. Brookfield that she "is my beau-ideal. I have been in love with her these four years—not so as to endanger peace or appetite but she always seems to me to speak and do and think as a woman should."[13] He writes of her in the same idyllic terms he used to discuss his mother, and she served as model for both Laura Bell and Lady Castlewood.[14] They filled a mutual need in each other's life: Thackeray was basically wifeless and Jane's marriage was a failure—after ten years of marriage her husband had grown cold, even cruel, and she and her husband were both saddened that they had had no children. As Ray states, Thackeray "meant hardly less to her than did her husband, while she had long been the center of his emotional life."[15] But eventually her husband lost patience with her intimacy with his friend, and he and Thackeray quarreled. Jane apparently ended her close friendship with Thackeray at her husband's bidding. As Thackeray dolefully remarked, " 'I have been played with by a woman, and flung over at a beck from the Lord and master.' "[16] He exorcised his grief and frustrations in narrating Henry and Rachel's troubled relationship in *Henry Esmond*.

Having suffered long separations from the three most important women in his life, Thackeray was particularly susceptible to revering the image of the Victorian ideal woman, which reflected his longings for a woman who would be completely, selflessly devoted to loving and caring for her family. He saw aspects of this ideal in his mother, his wife, and Jane and recreated them in the characters of Helen Pendennis, Amelia Sedley, and Rachel Esmond, but his resentment toward these women's inadequacies, their failures in their love for him, creep into the characterizations, too. Anger at his mother for sending him away when he was five, despair at Isabella's eventual inability to function as a wife and mother, and resentment of Jane for throwing him over at her husband's request all shape his characterizations of mothers in the novels, making them far more interesting than simple angel-in-the-house characterizations. Although Amelia Sedley, Helen Pendennis, and Rachel Esmond reflect in their behavior the advice of guidebooks for mothers such as those written by Sarah Ellis and Sarah Lewis, their conduct and their effect on those around them reveals both the powerful attractiveness and the flaws of the ideal.

Why Be a Good Mother?— The Effects of Mothering in *Vanity Fair*

It is customary to say that Amelia Sedley is the stereotypical Victorian "good" woman—and, of course, in her behavior, she is. But in her effect she is not. As Sarah Ellis advised the wives and mothers of England to do, Amelia devotes herself body and soul to caring for her child and relentlessly loving and honoring the memory of his father. Thackeray's descriptions of her mothering often seem like the embodiment of maternal guidebook advice:

> This child was her being. Her existence was a maternal caress. She enveloped the feeble and unconscious creature with love and worship. It was her life which the baby drank in from her bosom. Of nights, and when alone, she had stealthy and intense raptures of motherly love, such as God's marvellous care has awarded to the female instinct—joys how far higher and lower than reason—blind beautiful devotions which only women's hearts know. (*VF* 425)

Sarah Ellis, who wrote in *Mothers of England* that it is a "mother's sacred duty to . . . see that the fountain of love is kept fresh, and pure, and perpetually flowing," would be pleased by the adoration that constantly gushes forth from Amelia's bosom.[17] And as both Sarah Lewis and Sarah Ellis suggest, Amelia attends to Georgy's spiritual and mental development as well as his emotional and physical welfare. We see them praying together, and Amelia sells a favorite shawl from Dobbin to purchase Georgy's books for school.

But her devotion does not produce the sterling results that the guidebooks suggest. Georgy becomes haughty, overly proud, and egocentric. The narrator states that he "grew up delicate, sensitive, imperious, womanbred—domineering the gentle mother whom he loved with passionate affection. He ruled all the rest of the little world round about him. As he grew, the elders were amazed at this haughty manner and his constant likeness to his father. . . . He suffered his grandmother with a goodhumoured indifference" (465). Later, when Amelia has to give him up to Mr. Osborne, his paternal grandfather, he demonstrates no grief on leaving her, although the separation breaks her heart. A short stay with this grandfather teaches him that "his grandsire was a dullard; and he began accordingly to command him and to look down upon him" (649). Although he grieves when Dobbin leaves, he expresses little grief at the deaths of either of his grandfathers. The perpetual flow of love that Amelia unquestionably gives him produces a spoiled child with an inflated sense of his self-worth.

It would seem, given the results of Amelia's mothering, that Thackeray in this portrayal openly critiques the ideal mother that his times proscribed. And he finds fault with Amelia on more grounds than just the effects of her mothering. He frequently refers to her as weak and shows how others find her dull. In spite of the fact that her weakness attracts male admiration, particularly Dobbin's, she is unable to sustain her own husband's interest for long and eventually even the devoted Dobbin comes to see her inadequacies and in the end dotes on their daughter far more than on her. But in spite of what seem to be attacks on the feminine ideal as represented by Amelia, it is oversimplifying the picture to say that Thackeray deliberately undermines the angel-in-the-house image. His attitude toward Amelia is more contradictory and complex than that. He seems to feel that Amelia *is* the ideal, *is* what women should aspire to, but he throws up his hands at the perversity of the world for not responding to the ideal more positively. Ray points out that "Thackeray is himself the blindest worshipper of this domestic goddess."[18]

Thackeray's mixed attitude toward Amelia shapes both his introduction of her and his picture of her in the conclusion. For instance, in the beginning of *Vanity Fair* he cannot seem to make up his mind about whether she is or is not a heroine. In the first chapter, he writes that "she was a dear little creature; and a great mercy it is, both in life and in novels, which . . . abound in villains of the most sombre sort, that we are to have for a constant companion so guileless and good-natured a person." He adds that since "she is not a heroine, there is no need to describe her person" (43). But in chapter 2, in describing Becky in reference to the other ladies at Miss Pinkerton's, he comments that it cannot be expected that "twenty-four young ladies should all be as amiable as the heroine of this work, Miss Sedley (whom we have selected for the very reason that she was the best-natured of all; otherwise what on earth was to have prevented us from putting up Miss Swartz, or Miss Crump, or Miss Hopkins, as heroine in her place?)" (48)

Just as he cannot seem to make up his mind about whether or not Amelia is a heroine, so he has difficulties deciding whether or not she is the angel-ideal of a woman. Amelia remains the picture of the ideal devoted mother and loving, mourning wife until the conclusion, yet in the end when Dobbin finally loses patience with her and tells her she is not worthy of his love, it's hard not to feel Thackeray's judgment behind Dobbin's words. Thackeray encapsulates his mixed feelings about her most succinctly in one three-word description in the final chapter when he calls her a "tender little parasite" (792).

Ray argues that the contradictions in Thackeray's attitude toward Amelia stem from his having used his wife as the model for her character. His affection for his wife, his fond memories of their early courtship and marriage, led him to be overly generous in his commentary about Amelia, Ray feels.[19] No doubt this is at least in part true, but it ignores the fact that Amelia shares much in common with later characters such as Laura Bell, Helen Pendennis, and even Lady Castlewood, all modeled on other women in his life, and all sharing many elements of the same female ideal. In his characterization of Amelia, Thackeray suggests a strong perversity and contrariness in human desire. She is the ideal, she is what children, lovers, and husbands want, but even the ideal cannot satisfy. More than Becky's worldly machinations, it is Amelia's failures as a mother and wife, in spite of all her attractions and devotion, that inspire the narrator to exclaim in the last paragraph, "Ah! *Vanitas Vanitatum!* Which of us is happy in this world? Which of us has his desire? or, having it, is satisfied?" (797). Thackeray's portrayal of Amelia is such a strange mix of adoration and critique because with her, as with later female characters, Thackeray creates both the woman that he had most wanted and missed in his childhood and adulthood and the woman whose inadequacies and absences had so frustrated him. Amelia stems from more than poor Isabella Shawe; she grows from his most basic needs for and ideas about women, and from basic unavoidable frustrations embedded in all mother/ son relationships.

Readers' responses to Amelia have been as mixed as Thackeray's. Ray points out that many readers found Amelia a relief in such an acerbic novel, and John Carey suggests that after *Vanity Fair* Thackeray turned more to such portrayals to please the taste of the general readership and gain popularity.[20] But critics at the time did not necessarily reflect the general taste for sentimentalism. John Forster in the *Examiner* of July 22, 1848 referred to Amelia as "good and amiable but somewhat selfish and insipid."[21] In a *Spectator* review, Robert Stephen Rintoul commented unfavorably on the mixed portrayal of Amelia, whose "extreme attachment . . . to a selfish, worthless, neglectful young man, may be forgiven as *so* natural, yet the manner in which she yields to it, and nurses her sentiment to the neglect of her duties, as well as her subsequent shilly-shally conduct to . . . Dobbin, is rather mawkish than interesting."[22] Robert Bell in a *Fraser's Magazine* review was more sympathetic and found that Amelia's "pale lustre shines out so gently in the midst of [the] harpies." But even he stated that Thackeray "has made her patient and good, loving, trusting, enduring, [but] he has also made her a fool. Her meekness under suffering, her innocent faith in the evils which she lacks sagacity to penetrate constantly excite our pity."[23] Obviously the fictional embodiment of the Victorian female ideal won less widespread popularity than the ideal itself.

Winning much more critical acclaim from Victorian as well as modern critics is Becky Sharp, the antithesis of the ideal mother. Forster in his *Examiner* review remarked that "it is impossible to escape being charmed with the indomitable buoyancy, self-possession, and *aplomb* of the little adventuress, Becky, even while we are conscious of her utter depravity." And Rintoul, who had found Amelia "rather mawkish than interesting," opined that Becky is a "very wonderfully-drawn picture" although "too deficient in morale to excite interest" (apparently he felt the two characters were too extreme in their embodiment or lack of sentiment).[24] Thackeray, too, seems delighted with her in spite of himself, although he certainly condemns her many times over for her failures and cruelties as a mother, and these scenes are the most damning against her in the book.

Becky practices (or fails to practice) motherhood as if she were determined to rebel against every adage of the guidebooks for mothers, except for when she wishes to make a good impression on someone. As soon as little Rawdon is born she farms him out to nurse and rarely sees him, and the separation does not seem to disturb her in the least. In direct contrast to Georgy's taking Amelia for granted, Rawdon, as a young boy, comes to admire Becky as some distant goddess, and the fear of disturbing her in the morning enables him to stifle his cries when his father accidentally cracks his head against the ceiling in giving him a playful toss. As the narrator tells us, "she was an unearthly being in [little Rawdon's] eyes, superior to his father—to all the world: to be worshipped and admired at a distance" (448). The narrator details the boy's solitude in the house, his lonely dinners, his worshipful excursions to visit the wonders of her bedroom. "Oh, thou poor lonely little benighted boy!" the narrator exclaims, "Mother is the name of God in the lips and hearts of little children; and here was one who was worshipping a stone!" (449).

Thackeray condemns Becky in this picture of the boy's neglect and her heartlessness; he completes the picture in the terrible scene in which she boxes his ears for eavesdropping on her when she is singing for Lord Steyne. When little Rawdon runs crying to his friends in the kitchen he gasps out, " 'it is not because it hurts me . . . only—only. . . . Why mayn't I hear her singing? Why don't she ever sing to me—as she does to that bald-headed man with the large teeth?' " (522). It is the only time we hear little Rawdon openly complaining against his mother, a fact that further ennobles him and damns her. Usually he presents quite a stoical front, as when he has been left back in London while his parents stay at Queen's Crawley for the elder Sir Pitt's funeral and a long visit. His messages to them reveal none of the longing or loneliness that the narrator describes in his commentary. " 'I am very well,' " little Rawdon writes, " 'I hope you are very well. I hope Mamma is very well. The pony is very well. Grey takes me to ride in the Park. I can canter. Met the little boy who rode before. He cried when he cantered. I do not cry' " (495). The tone of the letter is very similar to the earliest letter we have of Thackeray's, written two weeks before his sixth birthday and sent back to his mother in India shortly after he arrived in England. "My dear Mama," he writes:

> I hope you are quite well: I have given my dear Grandmama a kiss. my [sic] Aunt Ritchie is very good to me [sic] I like Chiswick [sic] there are so many good Boys to play with. St. James's Park is a very fine place [sic] St. Pauls [sic] Church too I like very much [sic] it is a finer place than I expected [sic] I hope Captain Smyth is well. give [sic] my love to him and tell him he must bring you home to your affectionate little Son.

Underneath the letter he sketched a man on a horse.[25] The stoic tone—in spite of obvious reasons for fear and loneliness—the repetitions of well-wishing, the mention of the park, and the mention (albeit through a sketch) of horseback riding link this letter to little Rawdon's and suggest that Thackeray used some of his own boyhood experiences in depicting Rawdon. By extension then, Becky might reflect some of his deepest resentments of his mother for being cold-hearted enough to send him away when he was five years old. The clinging, devoted Helen Pendennis, more commonly associated with his mother, forms only part of the picture.

In spite of Thackeray's open condemnation of Becky's mothering, he rewards her deficiencies with a generous, gentlemanly, fair-minded son, a much more likeable son than Amelia's haughty Georgy. Little Rawdon is described as "generous and soft in heart: fondly attaching himself to all who were good to him," as opposed to Georgy, who scorns his grandfather and takes his mother's affection for granted (521). And although Rawdon would be justified in growing to hate his mother, who has treated him so cruelly and neglectfully, he never displays any such emotion. He declines to see her when he inherits the Crawley estate, yet he still makes her "a liberal allowance," which seems more than she would be bothered to do for him (796).

In more minor characterizations, Thackeray continues to undermine the picture of the angel-in-the-house as mother and wife. Lady Jane Crawley, for instance, is another Amelia in her meekness, kindness, devotion to children, and inexplicable admiration for her husband. But, like Amelia, the results of her wifely and maternal devotion are somewhat lacking. She produces a physically weak boy who is always sickly and dies young of whooping cough and measles, thereby leaving little Rawdon as heir of Queen's Crawley (another asset for Becky). And her husband, Sir Pitt, becomes bored of her like George Osborne with Amelia and is lured away by the fascinations of Becky.

The narrator's depiction of Mrs. Bute Crawley as a "virtuous . . . good and respectable mother" (467-68) more overtly satirizes the notion of good motherhood than the other characterizations do. Her children are models of talent and decorum, but the narrator reveals the behind-the-scenes picture that makes the success possible—an overly demanding mother, fiercely intent on successfully selling her daughters on the marriage market:

> Fanny and Matilda sang duets together, mamma playing the piano, and the other two sisters sitting with their arms round each other's waists, and listening affectionately. Nobody saw the poor

> girls drumming at the duets in private. No one saw mamma drill-
> ing them rigidly hour after hour. . . . Everything that a good and
> respectable mother could do Mrs. Bute did. She got over yacht-
> ing men from Southampton, parsons from the Cathedral Close
> at Winchester, and officers from the barracks there. She tried to
> inveigle the young barristers at assizes. . . . What will not a mother
> do for the benefit of her beloved ones? (468).

In this passage, Thackeray does not so much ridicule the maternal ideal
of contemporary guidebooks, which usually suggest how to *be* a good
wife more than how to *become* one; he satirizes instead the practices of
many mothers who felt it their duty to snag husbands for their daughters. The tone of this portrait of a "good and respectable mother" differs
greatly from that used in describing Lady Jane or Amelia. The ambivalence he creates around their characters is not there for Mrs. Bute Crawley.

In *Corrupt Relations,* Richard Barickman, Susan MacDonald, and
Myra Stark argue that contradictions in Thackeray's portrayal of women,
particularly Amelia, reveal his own ambivalence to the female ideals, and
they suggest that he finally bursts out of the tensions of the ambivalent
portrayal "into direct, unmistakable condemnation of the male-controlled
sexual system."[26] But there is rarely anything direct and unmistakable in
Thackeray's depiction of women, mothers in particular. The glowing
praises of the maternal ideals exist side by side with the accounts of their
failures; the two will not resolve. There is a longing, loving, albeit saccharine quality to these portraits that is as undeniable as the force of his
satire of the pretentious and hypocritical.

The authors of *Corrupt Relations* note that Thackeray's condemnation against the patriarchal system grows to a hysterical pitch in his dia-
tribe against male sadism in the passage in *Vanity Fair's* chapter 57 where
he describes women "stretched on racks in [their] bedrooms" (662), but
the authors admit that the narrator seems to take a voyeuristic pleasure
in describing the scene of torture. "These attitudes cannot easily be reconciled with each other," they comment.[27] That admission of irreconcil-
able contradictions seems more accurate than their earlier claim that he
bursts into "direct, unmistakable condemnation of the male-controlled
sexual system." Thackeray's portraits of women and mothers in particular frustrate and continue to fascinate because he never does resolve the
tensions within them nor does he ever overtly or clearly indict the social
expectations and conditioning that produce such women. Even when he
enumerates the weaknesses of his devoted mothers, the very weaknesses

themselves seem to excite him. He longed for and idolized the maternal ideal, while recognizing its flaws, sometimes critically, often adoringly.

Remaking Mother in *Pendennis*

Since Thackeray based Helen Pendennis on his mother, it is not surprising that he reveals in her both his adoration and his criticisms of the maternal ideal. Even more than in his portrait of Amelia, Thackeray with Helen Pendennis shows the dangers and attractions of the passionately devoted mother.

Thackeray's Oedipal tensions, particularly his anger at his mother's remarriage to Major Carmichael-Smyth, perhaps explain why he quickly dispenses with fathers and would-be fathers in *Pendennis*. Thackeray clears away Arthur's father before the end of chapter 2, when the boy is 16 and just starting to look for his whiskers to appear. The narrator reports that after the first shock of grief at his father's death is over, the boy feels "springing up in his breast a sort of secret triumph and exultation" (*P* 25). The only other male rival for his mother's affections turns out to be Arthur's tutor. When Arthur, also called Pen, finds out that his tutor has had the audacity to consider marrying his mother, he bursts out in indignation at his effrontery. " 'My tutor, I say *my tutor*,' " Arthur proclaims, " 'has no right to ask a lady of my mother's rank of life to marry him. It's a breach of confidence. I say it's a liberty you take, Smirke—it's a liberty. Mean, indeed!' " (193). He sends the grief-stricken tutor off and ends the evening with an intimate conversation with his mother "full of love, confidence, and laughter" (195). From then on no other male rival encroaches on his maternal terrain.

Gordon Ray presents in *The Buried Life* an excellent analysis of the parallels between Helen Pendennis and Thackeray's mother. As he puts it, Helen Pendennis is meant "to be a quite literal picture of Mrs. Carmichael-Smyth," and he quotes Thackeray's letter to Arthur Hugh Clough in which he states that " 'Mrs. Pendennis is living with me. . . . (She is my mother).' "[28] Ray indicates that in his portrayal of his mother, Thackeray captures both the angelic woman he perceived as a child and the more human woman who at times frustrated him as an adult, in spite of or because of their intense love for each other. In an 1852 letter he wrote that

> it gives the keenest tortures of jealousy and disappointed yearning to my dearest old mother (who's as beautiful now as ever) that she can't be all in all to me, mother sister wife everything

> but it mayn't be—There's hardly a subject on wh. we don't dif-
> fer. And she lives away at Paris with her husband . . . and a jeal-
> ousy after me tears & rends her. Eh! who is happy? When I was
> a boy at Larkbeare, I thought her an Angel & worshipped her. I
> see but a woman now, O so tender so loving so cruel.[29]

The diction and punctuation of this letter reveal something of his mixed, potent feelings toward his mother. His comment on her beauty strikes interest as it seems apropos of nothing and suggests that his feelings about her exceed traditional boundaries. Notice that he places no punctuation in the list "mother sister wife," which underscores how the roles blend together for both his mother and him (he follows the same pattern with "O so tender so loving so cruel," which emphasizes the confused blend-ing of these behaviors in his image of his mother). It is also worth noting that he refers to Major Carmichael-Smyth as "her husband" as opposed to "my stepfather." He seems to prefer appellations that distance him from his stepfather, such as in a letter that I quote later in which he refers to him as "the old gentleman." Thackeray clarifies the connection be-tween Helen Pendennis and his mother when he writes that, "My daugh-ter Anny says O how like Granny is to Mrs. Pendennis Papa—and Granny is mighty angry that I should think no better of her than that."[30]

Gordon Ray shows how Thackeray captures the tenderness and loving of Mrs. Carmichael-Smyth in the angelic, ideal Helen, and how he also recreates her cruelty in Helen's suspicions about Pen and Fanny, her mean treatment of Fanny, and her withholding of a letter from the girl to Pen. This fictional situation, Ray indicates, approximates Thackeray's real-life frustrations with his mother for unfairly suspecting him of having an affair with his children's governess.[31] Thackeray includes another of his mother's failings in his characterization of Mrs. Pendennis—her lack of a sense of humor. In an 1849 letter to Mrs. Brookfield, he refers to his mother as "Mater Dolorosa" and says that she "gloomifies me more than the old gentleman—I would die rather than make a joke to her."[32]

As Thackeray was living with his mother and stepfather during the writing of Pendennis, Mrs. Carmichael-Smyth's gloomification of him natu-rally cast its pall over the portrait of Helen, who incessantly seems to be wringing her hands or her hanky in concern and grief over Pen. But such excessive maternal concern and suffering constitute the role of mother in its holiest manifestations, according to Thackeray:

> The maternal passion is a sacred mystery to me. What one sees
> symbolized in the Roman churches in the image of the Virgin
> Mother with a bosom bleeding with love, I think one may wit-

ness (and admire the Almighty bounty for) every day. I saw a
Jewish lady, only yesterday, with a child at her knee, and from
whose face towards the child there shone a sweetness so angelical, that it seemed to form a sort of glory round both. I protest I
could have knelt before her too, and adored in her the Divine
beneficence in endowing us with the maternal storge [natural
affection], which began with our race and sanctifies the history
of mankind. (25)

When Mrs. Pendennis isn't wringing her hands or her hanky, she's often
praying. When Pen leaves for college, she goes to his empty room and
kneels beside his bed "and there prays for her boy, as mothers only know
how to plead" (200). In the reconciliation scene between her and Arthur,
it's Arthur who falls at her knees and recites the Lord's Prayer, with her
joining in for the last lines and conveniently dying moments later (736).

Helen's death scene resembles the passage in *Vanity Fair* that describes how every night and every morning Amelia and little Georgy say
the Lord's Prayer together, "the mother pleading with all her gentle heart,
the child lisping after her as she spoke" (*VF* 461). Apparently this tableau
had a real resonance for Thackeray, encapsulating as it does a physically
and emotionally intimate and private moment between a mother and
son in a bedroom, a scene charged with love, devotion, and holiness—
and a sentiment that makes most modern readers a bit queasy. In these
praying scenes, Thackeray echoes the sentiments of Sarah Lewis in *Woman's
Mission* when she writes that women have "no less an office than that of
instruments (under God) for the regeneration of the world,—restorers of
God's image in the human soul." Amelia and Mrs. Pendennis would agree
with Lewis that mothers "as the guardian angels of man's infancy are
charged with a mission—to them is committed the implanting that heavenly germ to which God must indeed give the increase; but for the early
culture of which they are answerable."[33]

Thackeray emphasizes the holiness of Helen and her mission by
having Smirke call her a "dear angel," Dr. Portman describe her as "a
sainted woman" (twice), and the narrator refer to her as "an angel, trans-
figured and glorified with love" (*P* 193; 528; 735). No satire colors these
highly sentimental scenes in Thackeray; the holiness of motherhood was
a creed Thackeray could believe in, at least most of the time, even when
recognizing the failures of mothers.

And Helen Pendennis does fail Pen in numerous ways. Her passionate
attachment to him and intensive concentration on him and on shaping his
future yield some negative results. He becomes spoiled, pompous, and

undisciplined. When he goes to Oxbridge, he takes for granted that he should have the best as he takes for granted his mother's money, until he has spent it all. He seems to assume that her assessments of his talent and intelligence are fact, until he fails his examinations. A little more uncertainty about his own worth would have helped him out in his first career at Oxbridge as it does when he returns to try for his degree a second time. But when he returns home after finally passing his exams, he falls back into lazy habits, mopes directionlessly, seeming to wait for some course of action to pursue him. Helen's obsessive wish for Pen to marry Laura also works negatively. Knowing that the marriage is his mother's wish, Pen cannot help but take Laura for granted, a fact that he is unable to hide and she is unable to ignore when he first proposes to her.

Pen is at his strongest, most active and independent when he's farthest away from his mother and under the influence of Warrington instead. He at least finds a vocation and some direction and stops moping. Perhaps it is the distance he manages to gain from his mother during this time that makes her so jealous of Fanny, so unangelic when she meets her, and so vehemently possessive. The narrator describes Helen's face as "hopelessly cruel and ruthless" when she first looks upon Fanny (657). She dismisses Fanny coldly and even closes the door on the Major and Laura, having "taken possession of her son" in his bedroom (657). Of course it is her cruelty to Fanny, her suspicions about Arthur, and her withholding of Fanny's letter to him—all of which stem from her excessive, possessive love—that cause the biggest rift between mother and son. Yet that rift, culminating in Arthur's speech condemning her actions, directly leads to the intense reconciliation scene detailed earlier, which leaves mother and son in each other's arms and praying as a prelude to the mother's death. Distances, or the threat of distances, seem to bring the two rushing back toward each other with increased intensity.

That equation—distance ultimately yielding more intense love—comes into play when Helen dies. One might think her death would liberate Arthur from her influence and her plans for him, but in fact she seems to influence him even more effectively from beyond the grave. She becomes "worshipped in his memory, and canonized there, as such a saint ought to be" (791). It is only after her death that Arthur comes to love Laura as his mother had hoped he would, and when she finally agrees to marry him, his first words are, " 'Come and bless us, dear mother,' " after which the narrator tells us that "arms as tender as Helen's once more enfold him" (941). It is at best an awkward union, if not an incestuous one, considering that throughout most of his life Arthur has referred to

Laura as his sister and what she most resembles is his mother. It is fitting that the narrator compares her entwining arms to Helen's, for in many ways she is Helen's surrogate. Helen raised her; they shared their devotion to Arthur; they were united in their condemnation of Fanny—united in everything, in fact, except Laura's rejection of Pen's first proposal of marriage, which deeply disappointed Mrs. Pendennis. Helen created Laura in her own image, molding her to do what she herself could not, marry her son.

Apparently Thackeray was aware that readers might find the marriage between these two almost-siblings questionable, for he begins the last paragraph of the novel by writing, " 'And what sort of a husband would this Pendennis be?' many a reader will ask, doubting the happiness of such a marriage and the fortune of Laura" (977). He goes on to describe the marriage in rather lukewarm terms, particularly for one given to the excessive rhetoric he bestows in praising Laura and Helen as pure, devoted angels. We are told that Laura, "seeing his faults and wayward moods—seeing and owning that there are men better than he—loves him always with the most constant affection" and she and his children "welcome him back with a never-failing regard and confidence" after "his fits of moodiness and solitude" (977). The best that is said of Pen is that his children and wife "have never heard a harsh word from him" (977). It's not exactly a glowing report, but in fact a surprisingly realistic one for the ending of a book with such strongly sentimental passages. The doubts one might have about the wisdom of Pen marrying the woman his mother told him he should marry—a woman who has been like his own sister— certainly are not alleviated by the subdued closing of the narrative. The tone of the last paragraph, in fact, relates more to *Vanity Fair* than *Pendennis,* particularly when Thackeray embarks on a litany of the injustices of the world:

> We own, and see daily, how the false and worthless live and prosper, while the good are called away, and the dear and young perish untimely,—we perceive in every man's life the maimed happiness, the frequent falling, the bootless endeavor, the struggle of Right and Wrong, in which the strong often succumb and the swift fail. (977)

He ends by calling for charity for Arthur, who with "all his faults and shortcomings . . . does not claim to be a hero, but only a man and a brother" (977). The marriage between Laura and Arthur, then, does not end the book on a triumphant note, as the culmination of their and Helen's wishes, but instead casts a somber shadow over the conclusion, leading to a reflection on the vanity of worldly wishes, on inadequacies, marred lives, and injustices. The subdued conclusion seems to be an indictment of Helen's influence, her vain attempts to live vicariously in her plans for a happy future union for her children.

Marrying Mother in *Henry Esmond*

I said at the beginning of this chapter that Thackeray's mothers are the strangest in Victorian fiction, but none is stranger than Rachel Esmond, Lady Castlewood. With her, the role of mother won't hold; she tries to fill it, but it keeps slipping away, and she slips into sister, lover, friend, enemy, eventually wife—anything but the maternal role she originally takes on.

Thackeray's other mothers reveal that we often want an ideal in motherhood that actually isn't much good for us or for mothers. His characterizations of Amelia and Helen Pendennis reflect both the advice of contemporary guidebooks for mothers and Thackeray's own emotional needs and tensions concerning his mother and his wife; they suggest that what was looked for and desired in a mother often was shaped by psychological patterns rooted in infant needs and sociological forces created in part by the proliferation of publications directed at women (and the popularity of a seemingly very maternal queen). All the authors I focus on in this study demonstrate the influence of the conjunction of the personal, psychological tensions surrounding mothers with the increasingly popular image of ideal motherhood, broadcast by an ever-burgeoning number of book and serial publications. But each writer reflects these forces uniquely, sometimes with open hostility, sometimes with overt avoidance of the issues; in Thackeray's case it is often with paradoxical, incestuous characterizations.

In *Henry Esmond* we can see the incestuous tensions that were implicit in *Vanity Fair* and *Pendennis* come to a head. Perhaps it is the awkwardness of Henry's relation to Rachel that accounts for the turgid narrative voice that mars the novel (the constraints of writing historical fiction naturally account for some of this stiffness, too). Thackeray himself found the book " 'dreary,' " in spite of the subversive implications of Henry marrying, as John Carey points out, "a composite bride, satisfying a whole range of masculine whims. He marries his mother, grand-daughter, pupil and mistress all in one."[34]

When Henry, at age 12, first meets the new Lady Castlewood, he sees her as a goddess or angel, which establishes her as the kind of mother ideal we've seen in Amelia and Helen. Their first encounter encapsulates in miniature the dynamics of their future relationship, for in this scene he seems to be as much attracted to her beauty as he is moved and comforted by her sweetness and protection. He looks "up at her in a sort of delight and wonder, for she had come upon him as a *Dea certe,* and appeared the most charming object he had ever looked on. Her golden hair was shining in the gold of the sun; her complexion of a dazzling bloom; her lips smiling, and her eyes beaming with a kindness which made Harry Esmond's heart to beat with surprise" (*HE* 49). His first response, then, suggests the range of roles she will play for him. In this scene she initially looks at him kindly, but when she realizes he is the bastard son of the late lord, she drops his hand and leaves, only to return later feeling penitent for having hurt him and, looking at him with

> Infinite pity and tenderness in her eyes, she took his hand again, placing her other fair hand on his head, and saying some words to him, which were so kind and said in a voice so sweet, that the boy, who had never looked upon so much beauty before, felt as if the touch of a superior being or angel smote him down to the ground, and kissed the fair protecting hand as he knelt on one knee. (49-50; ch. 1)

This movement—from kindness, to rejection, to reunion—reflects the dynamic of Rachel's relationship to Henry throughout the novel; she first raises him like a son, then rejects him (ostensibly for assisting her husband in a duel that leads to his death but also because she fears her growing feelings for him), and then reunites with him rather hysterically, first as a renewed mother-figure, then as a wife.

Gordon Ray draws interesting parallels between Rachel Esmond and Jane Brookfield. Thackeray's close friendship with William and Jane Brookfield underwent a crisis when William, out of jealousy, began abusing Jane and ordered her to cease communicating with Thackeray. Ray shows how Jane's disintegrating marriage corresponds with Rachel Esmond's and how Henry's feeling of betrayal and loss when Rachel is cruel to him in the jail scene reflects Thackeray's hurt and anger when Jane obeyed her husband and cut him off. Ray then suggests that in the rest of the novel that narrates Henry and Rachel's eventual union, Thackeray indulges in fantasies of what might have been had their circumstances been different.[35]

Ray's analysis is well supported and insightful, but it obscures ways in which Rachel is really an amalgam of Jane and Thackeray's mother. The dynamic between Henry and Rachel not only parallels Thackeray and Jane's relationship, but also reflects the relationship between

Thackeray and Mrs. Carmichael-Smyth, in that Thackeray as a boy first experienced his mother's initial love and devotion but then felt rejected by his mother when she sent him away from India, and then became reconciled with her later when she came to England. Like Rachel with Henry, Thackeray's mother in later life served as both his mother and the replacement for his wife. Rachel's irrational jealousy of Henry's interest in other women mirrors Mrs. Carmichael's possessiveness with her only son and the jealousy about him which "tears & rends her."[36] Also like Rachel, Thackeray's mother was given to an " 'almost romantic passion of feeling,' " according to her granddaughter.[37]

Thackeray's amalgamation of Jane and his mother in the character of Rachel is particularly interesting because it underscores one of the intriguing insights that develops through Rachel's characterization: the frightening similarity between adoration of a mother and adoration of a lover. As I've suggested above, Helen Pendennis suggests the same connection, but at least Arthur's eventual marital union is one generation removed from his mother. In *Henry Esmond*, Henry does marry the woman who in all but genetics is and has been his mother. The queasy closeness of these two kinds of relationships suggests that something is amiss in the expectations and idealizations of both female roles that they should be this similar and this confused. The intense physical and emotional closeness and perfection expected of a mother-and-son relationship lends itself too easily to the expectations of an ideal angel lover. Neither allows much room for realizations of flaws, humanness, individuality, separateness, or conflict. The desperate longing after perfect union with an angelic mother simply gets transferred to an intense longing after the perfect lover, and in Henry's case no transfer is even needed. If the psychological and social expectations of these female roles were more realistic, human, and distinct, such a transfer would be less likely. Mothers and lovers would be more differentiated and women perceived more as individuals.[38]

The confusion between the roles of mother and lover in the case of Rachel and Henry causes considerable pain for both. Her outburst against Henry for having been at the tavern where he unwittingly picked up the smallpox virus seems excessively cruel, considering Henry could not have known the danger at the time. Her anger can only be explained by her jealousy of his interest in Nancy Sievewright, about whom Lord Castlewood teases him. " 'Why was he brought in to disgrace our house? Why is he here?' " Rachel cries, " 'Let him go—let him go, I say, to-night, and pollute the place no more' " (120). The words are particularly crushing to Henry as she "had never once uttered a syllable of unkindness to Harry Esmond; and her cruel words smote the poor boy, so that he stood for some moments bewildered with grief and rage at the injustice of such a stab from such a hand" (120).

This scene marks the advent of Rachel's hysterical, erratic treatment of Henry, and it seems no coincidence that it begins as Henry indicates his sexual maturation by his interest in another woman. Her cruelty in the jail scene mirrors her behavior over the smallpox episode. She blames him for the death of her husband in a duel and will not take the hand he offers her when she enters. She blames him not only for the duel, but also for having destroyed her marriage over the years: " 'I lost him through you—I lost him—the husband of my youth, I say. I worshipped him: you know I worshipped him—and he was changed to me' " (205). She seems to accuse Henry of taking away her husband's affections, but her words also suggest that Henry took away *her* heart and that is why the love went out of her marriage. As if these accusations weren't enough, she says there is evil in him, and she wishes he had died when he had the smallpox. Her words "rung in Esmond's ear; and 'tis said that he repeated many of them in the fever into which he now fell from his wound. . . . [He] sate at the foot of his prison-bed, stricken only with the more pain at thinking it was that soft and beloved hand which should stab him so cruelly" (206). Once again Rachel's excessive blaming and harshness make sense only when one considers her repressed passion for Henry and her guilt for loving him. Oddly enough, in spite of the obvious Oedipal tensions surrounding his love for his mistress and his role in Castlewood's death, Henry displays little guilt or passion in this scene until Rachel finally looks at him "with a glance that was at once so fond and so sad" (206). The tenderness of that look, even though it comes after her statement that it would have been better off if he had died, perhaps suggests to Henry the real nature of her love for him, and it sends the man into a fit in which, "tossing up his arms, [he] wildly fell back, hiding his head in the coverlet of the bed" (206). In the throes of his fit he reopens his wound, passes out, and falls into a fever. The excessiveness and hysteria of both Henry and Rachel indicate the emotional tumult created by their attempts to deal with sexual passion within a mother/son relationship.

Rachel's later reconciliation with Henry aspires to an even greater frenzy than her condemnations of him had:

> She smiled an almost wild smile as she looked up at him. . . . "It is your birthday! But last year we did not drink it—no, no. My

lord was cold, and my Harry was likely to die; and my brain was in a fever; and we had no wine. But now—now you are come again, bringing your sheaves with you, my dear." She burst into a wild flood of weeping as she spoke; she laughed and sobbed on the young man's heart, crying out wildly, "bringing your sheaves with you—your sheaves with you!" (253-54)

Her fixation on Henry's "sheaves" would tip this scene into the realm of farce except that her outburst is surrounded by the most solemn rhetoric about how "the depth of this pure devotion . . . smote upon him, and filled his heart with thanksgiving" (254).

Rachel's angelic devotion is again the theme of the scene in chapter 10 of the second book where Henry, perversely, turns to Rachel to pour out his heart, sick with love—not for her, but for her daughter Beatrix. The narrator describes Rachel as "an angel of goodness and pity" (291). " 'I am your mother, you are my son, and I love you always,' " she tells him, seemingly sincerely (292). It is little wonder, after such gushings about the purity of Rachel's devotion, that Thackeray chooses to shut down the narrative posthaste once Henry and Rachel's marriage is announced, with only the barest of explanations about how they moved into their new roles with one another.

Interestingly, the brief explanation that Henry does offer for his relationship with Rachel suggests that motherhood is chiefly responsible for the shift in their relationship. Because of tension and alienation between Rachel and her two children, Frank and Beatrix, Rachel feels "severed from her children and alone in the world" (513). Henry seems to offer marriage as a way of pledging lifelong fealty between child and parent, the kind she has not received from her other children, and Rachel responds favorably to the offer of a home with a child who has vowed to stay with her. Thackeray does not even try to cast the proposal in a romantic light. He leaves the two behaving toward one another as loving son and devoted mother, except for the fact that they've agreed to make an official, legal change in their relationship with one another, not an emotional one. The fact that the novel was as popular as it was is astounding and indicates that Victorian readers perhaps were less disturbed by the confusion between the roles of mother and lover than most modern readers are. Reviewers were mixed in their responses to Henry and Rachel's relationship, John Forster finding it intolerable but George Brimley finding it triumphant, while George Henry Lewes left it to readers to decide.[39] But many, such as Anthony Trollope, considered the novel Thackeray's greatest work.[40]

In spite of all the pain, hysteria, and perversity of Rachel's relationship with Henry, she mothers him more successfully than she does her other children, with whom her saintliness is a bit oppressive. It drives away her husband first, then her children. She spoils Frank much as Amelia does Georgy or Helen does Pen.[41] Rachel is Thackeray's strongest statement both about the dangers of angelic mothers and their attractions.

Juliet McMaster discusses how Thackeray often shows that in the battle between good and evil "the parent who chooses the one is likely to determine the child's predilection for the other."[42] Yet Thackeray certainly does not advocate a mother choosing to be evil in order to propel her children into goodness. Once again, he seems to throw up his hands at the irony, vanity, and perversity of the world that such angelic perfection in a mother should not work to the benefit of her children. The one revision he might make, in the cases of Helen and Rachel in particular, is that their purity might be tainted enough to make them more forgiving. As McMaster points out, Beatrix, who reappears later in *The Virginians,* says of her mother that she " 'was so perfect that she never could forgive me for being otherwise. Ah, mon Dieu! how she used to oppress me with those angelical airs!' " (560). One can hear hints of Thackeray's complaints about his "Mater Dolorosa" in Beatrix's lament.

In a time of excessive expectations of mothers, Thackeray seems to have bought into these expectations, projecting them against the women in his own life and being disappointed when the images didn't mesh. He projects these expectations onto his characterizations of mothers as well, reflecting and contributing to the Victorian ideal of motherhood. But always his intelligence and keen observation forced him to show the fault lines in the image, the insidious negative effects of the angel, so that even when he most idolized her, even when he most revealed his own—and the universal—longing for such a perfect mother, he also was helping to topple her. The incestuous strain in his mother-characterizations in particular suggests the insidious dangers of the feminine ideal that was so abstract it failed to distinguish ideal mothers from ideal wives, which, in Thackeray's world, often leaves both mothers and sons strained, confused, and hysterical.

Notes

1. Richard Barickman, Susan MacDonald, and Myra Stark, *Corrupt Relations: Dickens, Thackeray, Trollope, Collins, and the Victorian Sexual System* (New York: Columbia University Press, 1982), 35.

2. Quoted in Gordon N. Ray, *The Buried Life: A Study of the Relation between Thackeray's Fiction and His Personal History* (London: Oxford University Press, 1952), 13.

3. Ray, *The Buried Life,* 13.

4. Nancy Chodorow, *The Reproduction of Mothering: Psychoanalysis and the Sociology of Gender* (Berkeley: University of California Press, 1978), 69, 109-10.

5. Quoted in Ray, *The Buried Life,* 14.

6. *The Letters and Private Papers of William Makepeace Thackeray,* collected and edited by Gordon N. Ray, vol. 2 (New York: Farrar, Strauss and Giroux, 1980), 361.

7. Ray, *The Buried Life,* 14.

8. John Carey, *Thackeray: Prodigal Genius* (Boston: Faber and Faber, 1977), 12; Ray, *The Buried Life,* 105.

9. *Letters,* vol. 2, 361.

10. Ibid., 440.

11. Gordon N. Ray, *Thackeray: The Uses of Adversity (1811-1846)* (New York: McGraw-Hill, 1955), 238, Plate X.

12. *Letters,* vol. 2, 197.

13. Ibid., 231.

14. Ray, *The Buried Life,* 86-93.

15. Ibid., 84.

16. Quoted in Ray, *The Buried Life,* 85.

17. Sarah Ellis, *The Mothers of England; Their Influence and Responsibility* (New York: D. Appleton & Co., 1844), 89.

18. Ray, *The Buried Life,* 32.

19. Ibid.

20. Ibid., 36; Carey, 18.

21. See John Forster, from a review in the *Examiner,* in *Thackeray: The Critical Heritage,* ed. Geoffrey Tillotson and Donald Hawes (London: Routledge & Kegan Paul, 1968), 55.

22. See Robert Stephen Rintoul, from a review in the *Spectator,* in *Thackeray: The Critical Heritage,* 59-60.

23. See Robert Bell, from a review in *Fraser's Magazine,* in *Thackeray: The Critical Heritage,* 64.

24. *Thackeray: The Critical Heritage,* 56, 60.

25. *The Letters and Private Papers of William Makepeace Thackeray,* collected and edited by Gordon N. Ray, vol. 1 (New York: Farrar, Straus and Giroux, 1980), 3-4.

26. Barickman, MacDonald, and Stark, 36.

27. Ibid., 36-37.

28. Ray, *The Buried Life,* 49.

29. *The Letters and Private Papers of William Makepeace Thackeray,* collected and edited by Gordon N. Ray, vol. 3 (New York: Farrar, Straus and Giroux), 12-13.

30. *Letters,* vol. 3, 13.

31. Ray, *The Buried Life,* 54.

32. *Letters,* vol. 2, 525.

33. Sarah Lewis, *Woman's Mission* (Boston: William Crosby & Co., 1840), 11, 30.

34. Carey, 21, 145.

35. Ray, *The Buried Life,* 82-91.

36. *Letters,* vol. 3, 12-13.

37. Quoted in Ray, *The Buried Life,* 50.

38. As I've pointed out in the previous chapter, Brontë's heroines often confuse mother/lover relationships, too, but since their lovers have not had as close a familial connection as is often the case in Thackeray, the sense of incestuousness is not as strong.

39. *Thackeray: The Critical Heritage,* 150, 142, 138.

40. Ibid., 165.

41. See Juliet McMaster, *Thackeray: The Major Novels* (Manchester, England: University of Toronto Press, 1971), 100.

42. Ibid., 102.

Chapter 6

Escaping Mother/ Motherhood in George Eliot

O it is piteous—that sorrow of aged women! In early youth, perhaps, they said to themselves, "I shall be happy when I have a husband to love me best of all;" then, when the husband was too careless, "My child will comfort me;" then, through the mother's watching and toil, "My child will repay me all when it grows up." And at last, after the long journey of years has been warily travelled through, the mother's heart is weighed down by a heavier burden, and no hope remains but the grave.
—George Eliot, *Scenes of Clerical Life*

This bleak description of a mother's fate from *Scenes of Clerical Life* may appear unnecessarily pessimistic, but it sets the tone for much of George Eliot's fiction, which seems designed as a warning against motherhood. In Charlotte Brontë's works we saw her heroines seeking out mother-figures and mothering positions while at the same time feeling ambivalent (like their author) about biological motherhood. George Eliot's protagonists (and Eliot herself) seem much more consciously determined to avoid biological motherhood, and they are far less interested in searching for maternal surrogates. Yet they still search, like Brontë's heroines, for nurturing roles to play in their communities. Only in the last novel of Eliot's career, *Daniel Deronda,* do the need and search for mother come to the forefront as they do in Brontë's novels, as if Eliot finally had given up fighting the pull of mother. When looking at Eliot's depiction of maternal figures and attitudes toward mothering over the course of her career, one can see that she recurrently depicts heroines who struggle to escape the confines of motherhood and who again and again succumb to it.

In " 'The Mother's History' in George Eliot's Life, Literature, and Political Ideology," Bonnie Zimmerman argues that

> there are two categories of George Eliot heroines: the productive and the sterile. . . . Women who step beyond the social and biological limitations of womankind, who desire to transcend the ordinary "lot of woman" by any means no matter how admirable, who defy sexual standards, who rebel rather than submit: these women are visited by the curse of sterility.[1]

Zimmerman poses Eliot as a moral judge in this assessment, sentencing heroines to childlessness for their crimes of rebelliousness. Although Zimmerman's analysis of the importance of mothers in Eliot is astute, she seems to miss the ambiguities of the characters' sterility and motherhood. Neither condition seems a curse or a blessing in Eliot. The ambiguities of Eliot's portrayals of sterility and motherhood account for the fact that Zimmerman sees sterility as a "curse" for heroines while Gillian Beer sees *pregnancy* as a curse from which Eliot shields her heroines: "George Eliot seems . . . to protect her heroines with fairy-tale ease against the curse of pregnancy within an unloving marriage."[2] Both Beer and Zimmerman at times ignore not only the ambiguities of Eliot's depictions of motherhood but also the psychological subtleties of characterization that suggest that her heroines are making *choices* to try to avoid motherhood. Eliot does not just bestow pregnancy and sterility as reward or punishment; she creates characters who, in many cases, make decisions that fend off pregnancy but who nevertheless eventually become mothers.

At the same time that Eliot focuses on struggles over mothering, she tries to downplay the role of mothers, suggesting at times that their role is ancillary. Zimmerman points out how many mothers in Eliot's works seem silly and weak—they "often act like children to their own daughters."[3] But with *Daniel Deronda*, Eliot comes to acknowledge the primacy of the mother/child relationship, the drive to discover mother, and the overwhelming need for mother-love—the need for an ideal harmony between two people like that of a fetus and its mother or in adulthood like the mystical union Jane and Rochester achieve in *Jane Eyre*. Her final novel seems to be a conscious study of mothers and their effect. It offers, in the characters of Gwendolen and Mrs. Davilow, an interesting inversion of the psychoanalytic pattern discussed in chapter 2, in which the infant projects its initial frustrations in life against its mother. Gwendolen and Mrs. Davilow escape many of the hostilities embedded in the mother/child relationship by refusing to play the roles tradition allots to them, as shall be discussed later. Zimmerman may see Mrs. Davilow as weak and immature, but Mrs. Davilow has made mothering choices that work for her.

Although Eliot's characterizations of mothers are never as vitriolic as Dickens's, she produced her share of mother monsters—Hetty Sorrel kills her baby, Mrs. Transome contemplates murdering hers, and Princess Halm-Eberstein abandons hers, while Mrs. Vincy does her best to turn out two spoiled children and Mrs. Tulliver alienates Maggie and shows a marked preference for her son (as do Mrs. Vincy and the otherwise idyllic Mrs. Meyrick). Pauline Nestor points out other failings of mothers in Eliot's fiction: "mothers acquiesce to a conspiracy of silence as they give their daughters up to be married."[4] Mrs. Davilow in *Daniel Deronda* and Mrs. Raynor in "Janet's Repentance" seem particularly guilty of such silence. Mrs. Raynor perpetuates the silence after Janet's marriage by not confronting her daughter about her abusive husband and her drinking problem. " 'Mother! why don't you speak to me?' " Janet finally wails, " 'you don't care about my suffering; you are blaming me because I feel—because I am miserable.' " In response, Mrs. Raynor offers her a cup of tea and suggests that perhaps her breakfast didn't agree with her. The only advice she gives is to submit, to which Janet retorts that she should have warned her about how brutish men could be (*SCL* 242).

Even when well-meaning and loving, Eliot's mothers are often curiously ineffective and strident. Eliot describes Adam Bede's mother, for instance, as the kind of woman who would distress her children with "her anxious humours and irrational persistence," and certainly she frustrates Adam with her self-indulgent, self-pitying laments as he tries to get work done (84). Mrs. Poyser, aunt and surrogate mother to Hetty Sorrel in *Adam Bede,* brims over with a certain practical wisdom and a plethora of clever comments. But she has a glance like a "freezing arctic ray" (118), and she nags and scolds frequently and at length, feeling, apparently, that those are her chief duties as a surrogate mother. We are told that she wishes "to do well by her husband's niece—who had no mother of her own to scold her, poor thing!" (128) Scolding, for her, is the sine qua non of motherhood. But it has little effect on Hetty, except perhaps to drive her even further from the life-style Mrs. Poyser represents. All of Mrs. Poyser's astuteness—to which the narrator frequently testifies—does

Hetty little good, as she manages to get pregnant and goes almost full term right under Mrs. Poyser's nose without her noticing.

Although Mrs. Davilow in *Daniel Deronda* is emotionally much closer to her daughter, she too suffers from some obtuseness—she is not overly observant or helpful about Gwendolen's moral dilemma in facing marriage with Grandcourt. Granted her love is crucial to Gwendolen, but she cannot be of much practical help nor even serve as a confidante to her.

Mrs. Garth presents one of the most positive portraits of a mother in Eliot, but even she grates, with her scoldings and her exactingness. She loves her husband and children, takes fine care of the household, and, like Mrs. Poyser, is rife with practical wisdom. But her world is narrow: she seldom leaves the limited circumference of her home and perhaps because of this there is something small, even mean about her at times, especially compared to her generous, wide-ranging husband. She is "apt to be a little severe towards her own sex, which in her opinion was framed to be entirely subordinate"; she's more indulgent with men, however, as are many Eliot mothers. Mrs. Garth also appears to be "a trifle too emphatic in her resistance to follies" (243). Even the best of mothers, then, can be partial in her judgments and wanting in her affections.

Then there is the way that many Eliot heroines manage to avoid motherhood. As mentioned earlier, Gillian Beer feels that George Eliot protects her heroines "against the curse of pregnancy within an unloving marriage."[5] Beer mentions Romola, Dorothea in her marriage with Casaubon, and Gwendolen as examples. Of course, Eliot can exercise such fairy-godmother power over her heroines at times, but she also subtly and overtly suggests ways in which the heroines manage to avoid motherhood through their own choices. The lack of pregnancy is not just good luck, as shall be shown later.

Eliot's distance from her own mother and her antipathy to falling into the confines of motherhood no doubt inform these mother and antimother characterizations. Gordon Haight describes the relationship between Eliot (Mary Anne Evans) and her mother: "her mother had never been very close to Mary Anne; her father was "the one deep strong love [she had] ever known.' "[6] The initial frustrations that infants direct against mothers for failing to meet their needs, frustrations that grow as the child tries to break free of mother to establish its own identity, would have been intensified for Mary Anne by her mother's long illness. Before Mary Anne was two years old, her mother gave birth to twins who died shortly thereafter; her mother never regained her strength. She did not have the energy to give much attention to Mary Anne, and consequently the girl was sent off to boarding school when she was five years old (the same age that Thackeray was when he was sent away). Her father was the one to visit her most often, and she stayed close to him until he died. In addition to her close attachment to her father, she was also devoted to her brother Isaac, although since he, too, was away at boarding school they could only see each other on holidays.

But even if Mrs. Evans had been well, she and her daughter might still have been distant. Haight points out the similarities between accounts of Mrs. Evans and the sharp-tongued Mrs. Poyser, who, as we've seen, equates scolding with mothering. He also compares Mrs. Evans to the inadequate and scolding Mrs. Tulliver, who does not understand Maggie and can do her little good (6). It seems, then, that temperament as well as health and geographical distance isolated Eliot from her mother.

Eliot's distance from her mother began a pattern for her (and her fictional characters) of turning toward men instead of women for support and intimacy, as Nestor describes in *Female Friendships and Communities*. First there was her brother Isaac and her father, then publisher John Chapman, philosopher Herbert Spencer, her long-term partner George Henry Lewes, and finally her husband John Cross. Later in life she told her friend Edith Simcox that she never much cared for women.[7] Interestingly, like one of Brontë's heroines, Eliot mothered many of these men with whom she was intimate. Yet she avoided biological motherhood—Haight reports that she used some method of birth control to avoid becoming pregnant with Lewes, and as Nestor points out, she " 'profoundly rejoice[d]' that she had never 'brought a child into this world.' "[8] Mothering grown-ups appealed to her, however, at least to an extent, perhaps because such a relationship was more intellectually stimulating than caring for a small child.

At the age of 16 when her mother died, Eliot took her mother's place in the family and cared for her father until he died in 1849. Later George Henry Lewes and his sons clearly recognized her maternal nature and called her "Mutter," "Mother," and "Madonna."[9] Much attention has been paid to how Lewes aided and protected Eliot in her writing endeavors, but she nurtured him, too, through the split with his wife, his arduous writing tasks, and his long illnesses. She nursed his grown son Thornie, too, attending to him throughout his painful and protracted death from tuberculosis of the spine. She also had a coterie of devoted women disciples who were like spiritual daughters to her and who often called her mother.[10] And John Cross, the man she eventually married, was certainly young enough to be her son; she referred to him as "nephew" in correspondence.[11] His proposal of marriage to Eliot, following closely upon the death of his mother to whom he was very attached, seems to have been an attempt to bind himself to another maternal figure. In their brief marriage, Eliot did end up mothering him; he had a fit of depression during their honeymoon in Venice and leapt from their balcony into the Grand Canal. She and his brother Willie cared for him closely as they made their slow way back to England. He recovered, but soon afterward she grew weaker, suffering from long-standing renal troubles. She died after three months of sickness and seven months of marriage.

Eliot's marriage was not the only mother-role she managed to get out of (or at least tried to), for in spite of her tendency to assume a maternal position in various relationships, she often came to find the role burdensome. So Lewes's boys, who on the whole she very much enjoyed, got on her nerves when at home for long periods of time. During one visit she wrote that she was " 'up to the ears in Boydom and imperious parental duties.' "[12] And she got irritated at Edith Simcox, one of her devotees, for calling her "mother" and did her best to wean the woman from her affections. Simcox explains that Eliot objected to the term because " 'her associations . . . with the name were as of a task.' "[13]

In *The Real Life of Mary Ann Evans,* Rosemarie Bodenheimer suggests that Eliot reveals her ambivalence toward mothering roles in her depiction of Daniel Deronda's discomfort in being a mentor to Gwendolen. He must endure confessions he does not necessarily want to hear, watch as his words of advice are misunderstood or not followed, and at times act more sympathetic than he feels. Bodenheimer concludes, "This is what happens when you put yourself in a position of moral superiority and wisdom and someone takes you up on it."[14] It is likely that Eliot experienced similar unpleasant feelings in her mothering roles.

It is little wonder Eliot thought of motherhood as a task, for she reached adulthood, as Gillian Beer notes, during a period when publications about women's roles and duties were rapidly increasing, and most of these affirmed self-sacrificing motherhood as woman's ultimate mission, as I've discussed in chapter 1.[15] Eliot was familiar with Sarah Lewes's *Woman's Mission* and the works of Sara Ellis and others that made exhausting, paradoxical, and impossible demands of mothers. But Eliot seemed to approve of their sentiment. She called *Woman's Mission* " 'the most philosophical and masterly [book] on the subject I ever read or glanced over,' " and she recommended it highly to her friends.[16] Then in an 1840 letter to Maria Lewis she mentions reading Aimé Martin's

L'éducation des Mères, "and I have found it to be the real Greece whence Woman's Mission has only imported to us a few marbles!"[17] (Sarah Lewis in *Woman's Mission* quoted extensively from Martin's work). Eliot refers to Martin as a " 'rational Christian' " in the same letter. Clearly at age 20, Eliot approved of both works and their traditional message to women. George Henry Lewes agreed. In an 1850 review of *Shirley,* he wrote:

> "the grand function of woman, it must always be recollected, is, and ever must be, *Maternity*: and this we regard not only as her distinctive characteristic, and most endearing charm, but as a high and holy office."[18]

He goes on to say that this high and holy office is not compatible with success in professions. Perhaps his conservative attitude toward mothering helped to maintain Eliot's, for even after she had abandoned many of the traditional religious beliefs of her youth, she still was touting traditional roles for women (while managing to escape them herself). In an 1867 letter she wrote that " 'woman seems to me to have the worse share in existence,' " but she felt that fact should lead to a " 'sublimer resignation in woman and a more regenerating tenderness in man.' "[19] The quotation sounds like it came straight from *Woman's Mission.* Yet while she seems to believe that it is necessary for women to be resigned, for mothers to be all selfless devotion, she also seems to regret that it is so, hence her belief that women " 'have the worse share in existence.' " Certainly motherhood appears an almost insupportable task if one accepts, as did Eliot, the script written by Sarah Ellis, Sara Lewis, and other writers of women's guides. If that's what she thought it took to be a good mother, it's no wonder she chose to skip it. In her own actions and, fortunately, in the female protagonists she created, Eliot was much less orthodox in her views of women's roles.

The Attempt to Flee Motherhood in *Adam Bede*

Many of Eliot's female characters seem to share her negative associations with mothers, for they do much to avoid becoming one. Both major female characters in *Adam Bede* consciously try to escape motherhood. The narrator tells us that Hetty finds the Poyser children "tiresome" and "the very nuisance of her life—as bad as buzzing insects that will come teasing you on a hot day when you want to be quiet." Little creatures of any kind have no charm for Hetty, although others interpret her plump, kittenish beauty as a sign of latent maternal affection. Mrs. Poyser sees past the deceit of her beauty and concludes that "her heart's as hard as a pibble" (200-1). Certainly when Hetty fantasizes about marrying Arthur Donnithorne she does not dream of conjugal bliss or loving children but of silk dresses and fine carriages and turning her neighbors and her aunt green with envy. As Mason Harris points out, these descriptions of Hetty suggest a "repulsion towards anything suggestive of birth or the maternal."[20] And of course when she does have a baby she says she " 'seemed to hate it—it was like a heavy weight hanging round my neck,' " and she abandons it to the elements (499).

In his insightful analysis of *Adam Bede,* Harris argues that Hetty is not the only one in Hayslope guilty of poor parenting. Mr. and Mrs. Poyser, although responsible, respectable, and virtuous for having taken over Hetty's care when her parents died, never really give her the love of a daughter but instead treat her more like domestic help. Hetty is the "outcome of the narrowness and complacency of their values along with their somewhat impersonal attitude toward her."[21] They instill in her a fierce desire to remain respectable, and Harris shows that it is this desire, along with her narcissism, that drives Hetty to kill her baby. She can face abandoning an infant to its death more easily than she can face shocking her community with her illegitimate child. Harris points out that the love of respectability drives Poyser to abandon Hetty just as she abandoned her child.[22] As representatives of Hayslope the Poysers and Hetty suggest that the community in general may be suffering from an over-zealous devotion to reputation and a lack of the kind of unconditional, forgiving—and maternal—love that Dinah Morris offers.

Dinah is the antithesis of Hetty in her love of her fellow creatures. She devotes her life to preaching and caring for others; her eyes seem always to be "shedding love" (67). Where Hetty may *look* full of maternal affections, Dinah actually is, and she is the only one to stand by and comfort Hetty in her imprisonment and through her aborted execution. Dinah's face is "full of sad, yearning love" as she looks on Hetty in prison. When they first embrace in jail, the narrator describes their reunion in prodigal-daughter terms: "Hetty, without any distinct thought of it, hung on this something that was come to clasp her now, while she was sinking helpless in a dark gulf; and Dinah felt a deep joy in the first sign that her love was welcomed by the wretched lost one" (493). Hetty appears like a helpless infant in this scene as she sits "clutching the hand that held hers, and leaning her cheek against Dinah's. It was the human contact she clung to" (494). Dinah is the perfect, placid Madonna, comforting the sinner forsaken by all others.

Yet, in spite of Dinah's nurturing impulses, she, too, resists the confines of biological motherhood by resisting courtship and matrimony. She casts her love fervently—but diffusely. She can pour her heart into a sermon to the villagers, making each feel she cares for his or her own personal salvation, but minutes afterward in walking home with Seth, she almost forgets he is even present (77). Seth pursues her hand in marriage even though he knows " 'a husband 'ud be taking up too much o' your thoughts' " (78). Dinah thanks him for his love but insists that her

> "heart is not free to marry. That is good for other women, and it is a great and blessed thing to be a wife and mother; but 'as God has distributed to every man, as the Lord hath called every man, so let him walk.' God has called me to minister to others, not have joys or sorrows of my own. . . . I desire to live and die without children" (79-80).

In spite of both women's ambivalence to having children, both succumb to motherhood in the end. By abandoning her child and allowing it to die, Hetty defines herself in terms of motherhood more completely than if she had had ten children and devoted her life to their upbringing. She commits the ultimate act of bad parenting, and her life afterward is shaped solely in terms of how she behaved in her brief hours of motherhood. Even a woman trapped in the limiting Victorian confines of husband, house, and children would have had more chance of having some life outside these connections than Hetty, sentenced to death for her crime, then pardoned and transported, severed from every human and geographical association she had known. In the epilogue we find that she dies on her trip homeward, so she never gets a chance to build a life that transcends her crime and punishment.

One of the wonderful ironies of Hetty's characterization is that after all the comments about her hating children and pets, all the instances of her narcissism, and her confession that she thought of killing her child and then abandoned it by a tree, she finally gets caught and condemned because she at last *does* experience irrepressible motherly feelings. Ultimately she can't escape mother-guilt. She keeps hearing her baby cry long after she is out of earshot, and the cry tears at her heart so that she has to return to the scene of the crime where she is found and arrested. " 'I did do it, Dinah,' " she admits, " 'I buried it in the wood . . . the little baby . . . and it cried . . . . I heard it cry . . . ever such a way off . . . all night . . . and I went back because it cried' " (497).

Hetty says she couldn't completely cover up the baby with grass and chips because she hoped someone might find it and take care of it. She runs, but when she "got out into the fields, it was as if I was held fast—I couldn't go away, for all I wanted so to go" (499). A man frightens her into leaving finally, but when she gets to another village she still hears the baby crying; even in her sleep the baby's cry follows her. " 'I turned back the way I'd come,' " she tells Dinah, " 'I couldn't help it . . . it was the baby's crying made me go: and yet I was frightened to death' " (500).

In the narration of Hetty's journey, Eliot suggests that even the most selfish, cold-hearted mother cannot escape the chains of maternal responsibility and guilt, which ultimately seem heavier and more deeply embedded in the mind and heart than survival instincts or concern for societal approval, although Hetty's desire for respectability, as I've mentioned earlier, motivates her initial abandonment of the baby. Hetty returns to her infant against her plans, against her will, against all sense of self-preservation, because of an instinct that drives her to mother the child in spite of herself. By acquiescing to that instinct, Hetty abandons all control over her own life. She establishes her identity as the woman who left her child to die and returned to be caught—there is no Hetty left outside this definition. Maternal guilt and maternal instincts, Eliot seems to suggest, are inescapable once set in motion and are more confining than all the outward limitations established for nineteenth-century mothers.

Dinah, too, becomes defined by motherhood, but in her case wifehood is included in the definition. In spite of her repeated vows to devote herself to others and not her own self or her own family, and in spite of her fears that her heart would not be "enlarged" by a husband and children, she finally agrees to marry Adam because her heart is divided without him (554, 576). Dinah gets as thoroughly entrapped in basic biological instincts as Hetty does. Her marriage to Adam seems as inevitable as the cycles of nature that govern the farm community of Hayslope, and, in fact, Eliot uses such farming images to describe how Mr. Irwine was "glad at heart over this good morning's work of joining Adam and Dinah. For he had seen Adam in the worst moments of his sorrow; and what better harvest from that painful seed-time could there be than this?" (578).

The epilogue gives a brief picture of Dinah as wife and mother—the kind of vague and hasty retreat once marriage and motherhood have been achieved that is typical of Victorian novels. But it is worth noticing that in the short epilogue in which we see Dinah, Adam, their two children, and Seth, Dinah's eyes and words are fixed far more on Adam than her children. The epilogue begins with Dinah in front of her house strain-ing her eyes toward the road to see if Adam is on his way home. Her first words are of him: " 'I see him, Seth' Dinah said, as she looked into the house. 'Let us go and meet him' " (581). She takes her four-year-old daughter by the hand to go out to meet him, and Seth brings the two-year-old son on his shoulders.

Although Eliot describes Dinah as looking fondly at her boy, she addresses no words to him as they walk along, nor does she touch him, and the only words she speaks to her daughter are her directions to come with her to meet Adam and later to " 'run to meet aunt Poyser' " (581, 584). She speaks only in the imperative to the girl. Dinah's attention seems to be consumed by Adam and the story he has to relate about Arthur Donnithorne. In Dinah's last words, the last words of the novel, she so-licitously requests Adam to " 'come in . . . and rest; it has been a hard day for thee' " (584). Granted, Eliot gives us only a brief picture of domestic life, but it is telling that she chooses to show Dinah's sights turned out-ward—toward the road, toward Arthur and Adam and their troubles—more than inward toward her children and home. The details are small but still imply that Dinah may find motherhood more confining than she'd like.

In the epilogue we find that Dinah has had to give up preaching because the Methodist Conference banned women from the role in 1803; she still does a little teaching in people's homes, but she's been denied the excitement and scope of those "happy hours [she's] had preaching, when [her] heart was filled with love, and the Word was given to [her] abun-dantly" (79). Eliot depicts what would be the perfect compromise for Dinah when Seth describes to Adam how Dinah took care of a young child while preaching. " 'There was a little thing happened as was pretty to see,' " Seth tells Adam:

> "the women mostly bring their children with 'em, but to-day there was one stout curly-headed fellow about three or four year old, that I never saw there before. He was a naughty as could be at the beginning while I was praying, and while we was singing, but when we all sat down and Dinah began to speak, th' young un stood stock-still all at once, and began to look at her with's mouth open, and presently he run away from's mother and went up to Dinah, and pulled at her, like a little dog, for her to take notice of him. So Dinah lifted him up and held th' lad on her lap, while she went on speaking; and he was as good as could be till he went t'sleep—and the mother cried to see him." (547-48).

In this tableau, Eliot envisions a perfect harmony of motherhood and vocation: comforting a child while preaching to the assembled community. Such harmony would be impossible for Dinah to sustain for long with her own children even if the conference had not forbidden women from preaching, for few children would sit passively while their mother preached. But if the tableau is read metaphorically, it suggests a blending of work and mothering that would be the most satisfying to Dinah, and perhaps to Eliot herself and many other Victorian women and their children, if such a blending were acceptable, or even logistically possible.

Questing for Large-Scale Mothering in Middlemarch

Like Dinah Morris, Dorothea Brooke resists biological motherhood in hopes of finding a wider world for herself; she still seeks out nurturing, service-oriented roles, but in her eyes—and, in part, in Eliot's—these roles are grander than that of "mamma." In the prelude and again in the finale Eliot makes the famous comparison of Dorothea and Saint Theresa, a woman defined not only by her great religious deeds but also by a vow of chastity that shielded her from the obligations of motherhood. The prelude prepares the reader for a story of a Theresa who finds "no epic life wherein there was a constant unfolding of far-resonant action" (3). Our Theresa, the narrator implies, will be a "foundress of nothing, whose loving heart-beats and sobs after an unattained goodness tremble off and are dispersed among hindrances" (4). The sentence ends, and "Book One: Miss Brooke" begins, making the connection between the hypothetical contemporary Theresa and Dorothea Brooke more obvious. But what are these "hindrances" that Dorothea's goodness gets dispersed by? The finale answers the question by describing Dorothea's life as wife and mother, half-apologizing for the conventional role she finally settles for. The narrator, then, equates family life with "hindrances," and Dorothea seems to agree, judging by some of the choices she makes in the novel.

Dorothea's resistance to motherhood is less conscious and less articulated than Dinah Morris's was, but still it is there. It is suggested first symbolically in the scene where Dorothea and Celia examine the jewels that have been left to them from their mother. Celia is eager to look at her mother's jewels and divide the plunder, but Dorothea has to be reminded and coaxed into examining them. " 'Dorothea dear,' " Celia pleads, " 'if you don't mind—if you are not very busy—suppose we looked at mamma's jewels to-day, and divide them? It is exactly six months to-day since uncle gave them to you, and you have not looked at them yet' " (11). Their mother's jewels, precious possessions hidden in a casket in a locked cabinet drawer, seem a symbol of female sexuality—female trea-sures, among which would be the ability to bear children. Celia is all for opening them up, exploring them, and trying them on. But Dorothea reacts to them at first with indifference. She puts necklaces on Celia and gives her advice on what to wear them with, but she takes no interest in wearing any of the items herself: " 'I have other things of mamma's—her sandal-wood box, which I am so fond of—plenty of things. In fact, they [the jewels] are all yours, dear. We need discuss them no longer. There—take away your property' " (13).

At this point Dorothea seems more than uninterested in donning her mother's jewels—she seems impatient with them, so much so that Celia feels "a little hurt" by her attitude (13). But suddenly a gleam of sun catches some of the gems in the ring box and catches Dorothea's interest, too. " 'How very beautiful these gems are!' " she exclaims, experiencing "a new current of feeling, as sudden as the gleam" (13). She takes par-ticular interest in an emerald ring and bracelet and decides to keep them, but not before she tries to justify her interest by associating it with reli-gious feelings: " 'It is strange how deeply colours seem to penetrate one, like scent,' " she muses. " 'I suppose that is the reason why gems are used as spiritual emblems in the Revelation of St. John. They look like frag-ments of heaven' " (13). Dorothea justifies taking the ring and bracelet, but Celia finds her inconsistency disconcerting.

The whole jewel scene foreshadows in miniature the course Dorothea will follow in resisting taking up her mother's jewel-roles—in particular marriage and motherhood. As with the gems, Dorothea first resists the temptation to follow the typical path. She doesn't want to don her mother's jewels, play her mother's role, and become a mother herself, so she marries an aging, ailing, enervated, bloodless scholar—a choice that might make birth control easy. She chooses to devote herself to his scholarly book and to community aid projects; she'll mother on a large scale, not a small one.

But Celia is right; Dorothea is not consistent. Her sudden attrac-tion to the jewels when the sun falls on them indicates a strong sensuous streak that can override her conscious, rational, and spiritual decisions. This moment of interest in the jewels foreshadows her passion for Will Ladislaw and how she is capable of changing her game plan with little warning—and how she searches through religious texts to find justifica-tion for her actions. In choosing to marry her husband's cousin, defy her family's wishes, and abandon what she inherited from her husband, Dorothea acts like a creature of passion, yet she would not have to search far in the Bible to find justification for choosing the traditional role of wife and mother, as she found justification for taking the emerald ring and bracelet. Dorothea's attitude toward her mother's jewels as they represent motherhood and sensuality prefigures much of her later responses.

One of Dorothea's exclamations in the jewel scene encapsulates a motif that runs throughout the narrative. When Celia suggests to Dorothea that they bring out the jewels, Dorothea agrees but suddenly exclaims " 'But the keys, the keys!' " and then "she pressed her hands against the sides of her head and seemed to despair of her memory" (12). The wording here seems particularly symbolic. She cannot remember or does not want to remember how to access the secret compartment that holds her mothers' jewels. Dorothea spends much of the narrative searching for keys—the key to being a useful, productive woman in a constricting society; the Key to all Mythologies that Casaubon is trying to write; the keys, finally, to being a good wife and mother and finding fulfillment in these roles. Celia, who all along has been eager for her mother's jewels and knows exactly where to find the keys to get them, eagerly embraces wifehood and seems to dote on both husband and baby (particularly baby). Her mother's jewels become her, and she enjoys wearing them.

Dorothea's ambivalence to motherhood becomes apparent in other symbolic scenes. Like Hetty Sorrel, Dorothea is not overly fond of little children or pets. When Sir James brings her a Maltese puppy she rejects it, saying, " 'It is painful to me to see these creatures that are bred merely as pets. . . . They are too helpless: their lives are too frail. A weasel or a mouse that gets its own living is more interesting. . . . Those creatures are parasitic' " (30). (Of course her feelings toward puppies reflect her frustrations with women's parasitic positions as well.) Celia had a terrier once, but it made Dorothea unhappy because she "was afraid of treading on it" (30).

Dorothea seems only to see lofty things—the little things get in her way and disturb her. She does not show much interest in Celia's baby either; she looks at mother and son "rather absently" (488). When Celia presses Dorothea to look closely at the baby's faces, Dorothea cries—and not out of happiness (489). She finds it "rather oppressive" to sit "looking rapturously at Celia's baby" (535). Granted, she feels if she could have been of service to the child, she would have liked it better, but ultimately the child bores her: "Dorothea would have been capable of carrying baby joyfully for a mile if there had been need, and of loving it the more tenderly for that labour; but to an aunt who does not recognize her infant nephew as Bouddha, and has nothing to do for him but to admire, his behaviour is apt to appear monotonous, and the interest of watching him exhaustible" (535).

While Dorothea resists biological motherhood, at least at first, she still seeks nurturing, caretaking roles in and around Middlemarch, ones that transcend the limited range of a biological mother. The narrator states that Dorothea's mind

> yearned by its nature after some lofty conception of the world which might frankly include the parish of Tipton and her own rule of conduct there; she was enamored of intensity and greatness, and rash in embracing whatever seemed to her to have those aspects; likely to seek martyrdom, to make retractions, and then to incur martyrdom after all in a quarter where she had not sought it. (8)

She wants to give of herself but give to something larger than the commonplace sacrifice of motherhood (although as the narrator warns us, she ends up incurring martyrdom in just the area she thought she'd avoid). When we first see Dorothea, she has just come from observing an infant school that she had established in the village, and she has taken up drawing plans for some buildings, probably the cottages she discusses with Sir James Chettam a few pages later. So, in the first specific descriptions we get of Dorothea after general commentary about her, she is taking care of children and homemaking. But, of course, both are done on a grander scale than is usual for women. She approaches both roles professionally and intellectually in terms of bettering the whole community as an educator and architect.

When she marries Casaubon, she marries his work more than the man, hoping to foster his studies and writings like one of John Milton's daughters. Having children with him never seems to occur to her. She talks of "devoting herself to him" and "of learning how she might best share and further all his great ends" (50); she never discusses the family they will raise together.

Yet Dorothea does not just want to serve for service's sake or to learn for the sake of knowledge alone: she wants to produce, if not children, then books. She becomes disillusioned with Casaubon when she sees his labyrinthine notes accumulating without getting any closer to a book—a creation of theirs that could go out into the world on its own. Dorothea wants to be part of this labor and delivery process, but the book is stillborn. Casaubon suffers from severe writer's block—he can't leave off note-taking and take up composition. " 'All your notes,' "

Dorothea asks, " 'all those rows of volumes—will you not now do what you used to speak of?—will you not make up your mind what part of them you will use, and begin to write the book which will make your vast knowledge useful to the world? I will write to your dictation, or I will copy and extract what you tell me: I can be of no other use.' " Dorothea ends her plea in tears, frustrated by his and her unproductivity (199-200). Eliot often referred to her own works as her children, and she invested Dorothea with a similar desire to produce this kind of offspring.[23]

Dorothea finds other projects to invest her time, energy, and money in, such as the hospital and helping to support Lydgate and Rosamond in their troubles. We see Dorothea expend far more energy and excitement in any of her projects, whether it be building cottages or clearing Lydgate's name, than in mothering her children, for the narrator pulls so far back from Dorothea in the finale where we discover that she has become a mother that she hardly seems present. We get no specific picture of her or words from her; we simply learn that she and Will have children who visit Celia and Sir James's children and that Will gets returned to Parliament with much "wifely help" from Dorothea.

The most specific picture of Dorothea's mothering that Eliot gives us is the scene where Celia finds out in a letter that Dorothea has had a child, and she wails because she thinks Sir James won't let her visit her and she's sure that Dorothea " 'will not know what to do with the baby—she will do wrong things with it' " (836-37). Zimmerman claims that in Eliot "women who do not rebel [against traditional women's roles]—or, more typically, who suffer and then submit—are blessed for their womanly wisdom by becoming the radiating center of a quasi-mystical family circle."[24] But the only thing mystical about the circles that form around Dinah and Dorothea are their vagueness. Both depictions entail a sense of loss.

In the Penguin edition introduction to *Middlemarch*, Rosemary Ashton suggests that the finale is more positive than the prelude because Eliot counters the negative adjectives that describe Dorothea's position with positive ones and emphasizes the good Dorothea has done for others. But Ashton does not comment on the effect of the final word of the book, "tombs": "that things are not so ill with you and me as they might have been, is half owing to the number who lived faithfully a hidden life, and rest in unvisited tombs" (838). "Hidden," "unvisited," and "tombs" dominate the last line of the book, making the ending tone somber, full of a sense of isolation and diminishment, especially when compared to the last words of the prelude, "some long-recognizable deed" (4). (It is worth noting that Eliot also refers to Casaubon's dreary Key to all Mythologies as

a "tomb," which suggests she sees some connection between his unpro-
ductive project and Dorothea's final fate [493].) Certainly, Eliot does
not suggest that Dorothea's family life is a disaster—it seems full and
worthy—yet it still appears a falling-off from her larger schemes of
mothering.

Rosamond Vincy, like Dorothea, also does not seem inspired by
the prospects of motherhood. The idea of marrying Lydgate attracts her
because of the prestige it will bestow on her since he is from outside
Middlemarch and has noble relatives. The prospect of buying elegant
housewares interests her, too. The maternal impulse comes in a distant
third—if it comes in at all. She brings on a miscarriage by going out
riding when Lydgate strenuously warned against it. When he first finds
out she has been riding, "after the first almost thundering exclamations
of astonishment," he says, " 'You will not go again, Rosy; that is understood. If it were the quietest, most familiar horse in the world, there
would always be the chance of accident' " (584). But she goes out again
anyway because she wants to be seen with Captain Lydgate, Sir Godwin's
son, and she wishes to advance her connection with his family. She shows
no concern at all about risking the loss of the baby, only a little concern
about running into her husband.

Rosamond demonstrates little concern or grief after the miscarriage
either, refusing to admit that the riding accident caused the miscarriage.
Mrs. Vincy remarks, " 'I'm sure I felt for her being disappointed of her
baby; but she got over it nicely' " (569). No wonder—in her mind, it
seems, there was not much to "get over." Zimmerman refers to Rosamond's
miscarriage as "an obvious metaphor for her remorseless egoism."[25]

Rosamond does become a mother, eventually, but all the narrator
tells us about her mothering is that "she made a very pretty show with
her daughters, driving out in her carriage" (835). This picture captures
what Rosamond would seem to value most in motherhood—being able
to use her daughters as additional ornaments to herself, extensions of her
home world that can be displayed to incite envy in the neighbors.

Mary Garth presents the most positive image of motherhood in
the novel—even more so than her mother. The finale informs the readers that Fred and Mary "achieved a solid mutual happiness" and had three
boys for whom Mary writes and publishes a little book, *Stories of Great
Men, Taken from Plutarch*. Unlike Dorothea, then, Mary manages to merge
motherhood with other creative pursuits. Mary seems to be a more relaxed parent than her mother and doesn't give her boys formal teaching
as her mother did, but they do quite well when they go to school anyway

"because they'd liked nothing so well as being with their mother" (834). Her ease with them makes her a successful parent. The narrator leaves us with an idyllic picture of Mary and Fred in their old age: "Fred and Mary still inhabit Stone Court . . . the creeping plants still cast the foam of their blossoms over the fine stone-walls into the field where the walnut-trees stand in stately row—and . . . on sunny days the two lovers who were first engaged with the umbrella-ring may be seen in white haired placidity at the open window" (834). Mary, with her intelligence, gentle temper, and nurturing instincts, excels in the art of making husband, children, and herself happy.

Mary's secret seems to be moderation. She's kind and loving but not saccharine, intelligent but not overly intellectual, hardworking but not driven. Eliot's other characterizations of mothers in the novel form an extended critique of excess: Celia is a loving mother but dotes on her baby to the point of absurdity, Mrs. Garth can be too severe and practical, Mrs. Farebrother can be too loquacious and domineering, Mrs. Vincy is excessively materialistic as is her daughter Rosamond, and Dorothea can be seen as excessive in her goals and expectations of herself. If she hadn't wanted so much, she (and we) could have been happier with what she got. But of course it is Dorothea's excesses that make her interesting and novel-worthy. A novel with Mary Garth as the protagonist would most likely be a bore. Still, Eliot poses Mary's moderation of temperament and goals, and her relaxed approach to parenting, as the secret of success for mothers, but as her own characterizations suggest, such moderation cannot be achieved by most women, nor would many even want it.

Daniel Deronda: The Search for Mother and Beyond

"I have thought of you more than of any other being in the world."
    —George Eliot, Daniel Deronda

As we've seen, the female protagonists in most of Eliot's works avoid motherhood—willfully or otherwise. All three stories in Scenes of Clerical Life reflect this pattern, as Sandra Gilbert and Susan Gubar point out.[26] Caterina Sarti in "Mr. Gilfil's Love-Story" dies in childbirth, Milly Barton in "The Sad Fortunes of the Reverend Amos Barton" dies similarly, and Janet of "Janet's Repentance" never becomes a biological mother, although she does adopt. Gilbert and Gubar see all three women as angels of death in their self-renunciation and their connections with deathbeds. They seem more allied with death than life. In Adam Bede we've seen how both

Dinah and Hetty resist motherhood but eventually succumb. And Dorothea and Rosamond in *Middlemarch* both take actions suggestive of resisting motherhood. Along with this pattern, Eliot has repeatedly suggested that mothers are of secondary importance, often nuisances, rarely positive guides. Eliot's heroines don't seek out maternal surrogates as Brontë's and Dickens's did. But in *Daniel Deronda,* Eliot disrupts these patterns. Granted Gwendolen does want, like the preceding heroines, to avoid motherhood, but otherwise the novel is dominated by the theme of mother-seeking and mother-pleasing. Far from being ancillary, mothers become the great motivators of action in this novel. Both Zimmerman and Beer note the prominence of mother themes in *Daniel Deronda.*[27] As Beer states, "the search for the mother becomes a binding theme," but she goes on to say that "it is a search which can never be fulfilled."[28] I would argue that the search is fulfilled better in *Daniel Deronda* than in any other major Victorian novel.

In *Daniel Deronda* Eliot depicts three major characters searching or longing for their mothers: Daniel, Mirah, and Gwendolen. Daniel and Mirah both have experienced early separation from their mothers but through inverse means—Daniel was sent away by his mother, and Mirah was stolen away from hers. Gwendolen, on the other hand, has an unnaturally close but not always positive relationship with her mother and experiences a great need for her presence after Grandcourt has died in Italy. Through the course of the novel, Daniel finds the mother who rejected him, Gwendolen is restored to a loving mother in an improved mother-daughter relationship, and Mirah finds out that her mother is dead. The three situations encapsulate the main possibilities in a mother: either she is rejecting, loving, or dead.

Daniel, who had entertained many sentimental notions about who his mother was, makes a journey to meet her finally, but even after they've met, she remains an enigma that he needs to search and explore. She bequeaths to him his Jewish heritage, which becomes to him a mother religion that also must be explored. As Zimmerman states, Deronda eventually finds his mother in his religion, "a curious idealization of Judaism as the 'heart of mankind,' 'the core of affection,' the 'well of mercy.' "[29] As she points out, these phrases are "all receptive, or passive, 'inner space' metaphors for the tender, nurturing mother."[30]

Deronda's disappointment, anger, and feelings of rejection upon meeting his mother, Princess Halm-Eberstein, fuel his embracing of Judaism and its most immediate representatives in his life, Mordecai and Mirah. Although the princess demonstrates some concern for Daniel and approves of his look, manner, and intelligence, their meeting does not live up to his dreams: "He had lived through so many ideal meetings with his mother, and they had seemed more real than this. . . . She kissed him on each cheek, and he returned her kisses. But it was something like a greeting between royalties" (687). Even before they meet, she has become to him more distant in his affections because he realizes upon getting her letter that she is not the wronged, neglected woman he has always yearned after in his heart (681). Still, when he meets her his first words are " 'I have thought of you more than of any other being in the world' " (687). When she tells him that in the excitement and fulfillment of her singing and acting career she "did not want a child" (689) the bold-faced rejection leaves him "clutching his coat-collar as if he were keeping himself above water by it" (689). A few moments later she reveals that he is a Jew, and he embraces the fact with an enthusiasm that surprises even him and seems to be inspired in "impulsive opposition to his mother," who had tried to free him from being raised a Jew (690). In other words, maternal rejection spurs him to cling to a religion that can nurture him.

The pattern is repeated later in the conversation between Daniel and his mother, when Daniel cries, " 'Mother! take us all into your heart—the living and the dead. . . . Take my affection.' " She responds by looking at him "admiringly rather than lovingly . . . and saying sadly, 'I reject nothing, but I have nothing to give.' " Deronda blanches under "the pain of repulsed tenderness" (697). His mother repeats her admission that she " 'did not wish [him] to be born' " (697). After she explains how she handed over Daniel to Sir Hugo Mallinger so that " 'you should not know you were a Jew,' " Daniel again welcomes his Jewishness by saying " 'And for months events have been preparing me to be glad that I am a Jew' " (698). His eager acceptance of his Jewishness serves both to ease his own pain at his mother's rejection and to wound and frustrate his mother.

Eliot repeats the pattern once again in the next conversation between Daniel and his mother, in which the princess rejects Deronda's desire to play the role of son to her; her cold response leads to his most vehement articulation of his loyalty to his race: " 'I consider it my duty—it is the impulse of my feeling—to identify myself, as far as possible, with my hereditary people, and if I can see any work to be done for them that I can give my soul and hand to, I shall choose to do it' " (724). Certainly Mordecai and Mirah have helped to prepare him for this realization of his vocation, but the vocation takes shape and gathers fire in response to his mother's rejection, as a way of opposing her and healing the wound she has inflicted.

The princess, of course, defies all norms of motherhood in thought, feeling, and behavior. She recognizes this and speaks passionately against the limits of the norms she has defied: " 'Every woman is supposed to have the same set of motives, or else to be a monster. I am not a monster, but I have not felt exactly what other women feel—or say they feel, for fear of being thought unlike others' " (691). Eliot seems to speak through the princess at this point, arguing that some women's passions and goals necessitate a life different than the one that *Woman's Mission* proscribed; some need a maverick life like Eliot's, the kind Dorothea hoped to have. The princess is a Dorothea with a better defined and trained talent and more nerve and independence. Certainly Eliot criticizes and punishes the princess's lack of human sympathy and compassion—fundamentals to Eliot's ethic—but through her she also criticizes once again the constraints that force a woman to sacrifice vocation for motherhood or motherhood for vocation. Eliot has it both ways in this characterization—she suggests that the princess is paying the price in guilt and pain for her bad mothering, yet she also condemns the injustice of a society that thwarts the drives and dreams of women like the princess who have no desire ever to be mothers. Deronda, reflecting, it seems, Eliot's ambivalent attitude toward the princess, tries hard not to blame his mother, and for the most part he is successful in quelling his anger and resentment, perhaps because he sees she is undergoing great pain, and is being withered away by her illness; he doesn't need to add any punishments of his own.

Having lost his image of a loving but wronged mother, and having learned from her that he was not and is not wanted, Deronda turns to other maternal ideals for consolation—Mordecai, Mirah, and Judaism—and they prove much more fulfilling. Mordecai is often depicted as maternal. He comforts the young Jacob when he cries: "this sign of childish grief at once recalled Mordecai to his usual gentle self . . . with maternal action he drew the curly head towards him and pressed it tenderly against his breast" (535). In chapter 40, Eliot describes him as having something of "the slowly dying mother's look when her one loved son visits her bedside, and the flickering power of gladness leaps out as she says, 'my boy!'—for the sense of spiritual perpetuation in another resembles that maternal transference of self" (553). Eliot depicts Mordecai as the spiritual mother of Deronda, giving birth to his new life. " 'You will be my life,' " Mordecai asserts, " '[my vision] will be planted afresh; it will grow. You shall take the inheritance' " (557). Mordecai's fervor and devotion help to make up for the princess's coldness.

Mirah, too, is depicted as having a strong maternal streak in addition to a longing for her own mother. She tells Mrs. Meyrick that she " 'would rather be with you than with any one else in the world except my mother,' " and she tells Deronda that she would like to find her mother to let her know that she always loved her (419). Like Deronda, Mirah desires to take care of her lost parent, to mother her mother: " 'if she is alive,' " Mirah says, " 'I want to comfort her' " (419), and later, " 'Oh, if we ever do meet and know each other as we are now, so that I could tell what would comfort her—I should be so full of blessedness, my soul would know no want but to love her' " (420). Mirah's mother is dead, so she never gets a chance to comfort her as she longs to do, but she does get a chance to mother her consumptive brother, Mordecai. In fact the first words she speaks after Deronda proposes to her are " 'Let us go and comfort Ezra' " (863). He dies in both of their arms.

Like Daniel and Mirah, Gwendolen has a desire to take care of her mother, but in her case she actually gets the opportunity to do so. In many scenes, Gwendolen seems more like the mother than the daughter. In chapter 9, Gwendolen makes her mother cry by criticizing the way she raised her, and when her mother bursts into tears, Gwendolen comforts her. Mrs. Davilow defends her subordinate position by saying that Gwendolen's will " 'was always too strong for me' " (129). When the family is struck by an economic crisis, Gwendolen again dries her mother's tears and takes charge (271). When Herr Klesmer gives Gwendolen his negative verdict about her talents, her disappointment and humiliation make her so grim that she scares her mother and once again ends up comforting her, although less tenderly this time: " 'We must try not to care. . . . We must not give way. I dread giving way. Help me to be quiet' " (309). The narrator states that Mrs. Davilow "was like a frightened child under her daughter's face and voice: her tears were arrested and she went away in silence" (309). Gwendolen's desire to help her mother partly explains her decision to marry Grandcourt, whose money can alleviate her family's poverty. Of course her own desire for position and possessions motivate her as well, but as she tells Deronda, " 'I really did think a good deal about my mother when I married. I *was* selfish, but I did love her, and feel about her poverty; and what comforted me most at first, when I was miserable, was her being better off because I had married' " (836-37). Her mother's comforts are chiefly in her mind as she decides how much of her inheritance from Grandcourt she should keep.

Gwendolen and Mrs. Davilow have inverted the typical mother/ child power relationship, thereby evading some of the frustrations that psychoanalysts have seen as inevitable in mother-dominated childrearing. According to Dorothy Dinnerstein, "through woman's jurisdiction over child's passionate body, through her control over what goes into it and what comes out of it, to withhold pleasure or inflict pain until it obeys her wishes, each human being first discovers the peculiarly angry bitter-sweet experience of conscious surrender to conscious, determined out-side rule." Dinnerstein concludes that children's frustrations with this rule, and with their mothers' failures to meet their demands, lead them even as adults to harbor resentments against women and to try to control female authority.[31] But Gwendolen's mother does not exercise authority over her daughter, nor does she frustrate her daughter's demands, unless she absolutely can't avoid it. As she herself says, Gwendolen's will has been too much for her. Because she has relinquished the authority to Gwendolen there is a greater intimacy and affection between the two than can be found in most mother/daughter pairs in Eliot's fiction. They even sleep together in the same room (53).

But the relationship between Gwendolen and her mother leaves Gwendolen in stasis emotionally. She's trapped in infant narcissism be-cause her mother *hasn't* frustrated her enough. As Nancy Chodorow ex-plains, identity begins with the frustration of primary love, and rejection by the mother serves to disturb the infant's "naive egoism."[32] Without such rejection and frustration, Gwendolen cannot mature; she controls her family, but often more as a willful child than a rational adult. And although she is close to her mother, she cannot confide in her about Grandcourt's relationship with Mrs. Glasher or the circumstances sur-rounding his death.

Deronda seems to be one of the first to truly frustrate Gwendolen into questioning herself. It is his judgment of her and her own disastrous marriage and separation from her mother that bring about Gwendolen's emotional evolution. Ironically, the evolution begins with what seems to be a regression into complete childish dependence. After she emerges from the Genoese waters in which Grandcourt has drowned, she clings to Deronda like a little child, while he sends for her mother because he remembers that she "had spoken of her mother's presence as a possible help, if she could have had it" (751). The narrator refers to her "childlike beseeching" as she confesses to Deronda, and he takes her hand "as if they were going to walk together like two children" (754, 755). She clings to her mother, too, when she arrives, and Mrs. Davilow relishes the op-portunity to mother her:

> Mrs. Davilow, indeed, though compelled formally to regard this
> time as one of severe calamity, was virtually enjoying her life
> more than she had ever done since her daughter's marriage. It
> seemed that her darling was brought back to her not merely
> with all the old affection, but with a conscious cherishing of her
> mother's nearness, such as we give to a possession that we have
> been on the brink of losing. (824)

In this state of dependence, Gwendolen faces her sins and weaknesses as
well as the terror of what she sees as her guilt in Grandcourt's death, and
she finally begins to mature. A greater equality has been established in
her relationship with her mother. She cherishes her mother's comforting
presence, but she also wants to make her happy. She no longer dominates all their interactions. And her recognition of her own failings in
marriage perhaps helps her to understand and forgive her mother's failed
marriage. Both are women who have married unwisely and lost much;
their similarly sad fates bind them more closely together.

In the end, Deronda is left with his nurturing religion and a maternal, loving wife, whom he can care for as he'd hoped to care for his
mother. Mirah cannot care for her mother, as she'd wished, but she is left
to love and be loved by the man who will carry on her brother's vision.
The narrator does not state whether or not she and Daniel have any
children. Gwendolen, who "shall be better" because she has known
Deronda, is left with enough money to care for her mother and sisters in
the home in which they'd been happy before her marriage. And because
Gwendolen managed to avoid getting pregnant, which is about the only
thing that went right in her marriage, Grandcourt's son by his former
lover, Mrs. Glasher, inherits the bulk of his property, which eases
Gwendolen's conscience. Of course, Gwendolen's avoidance of pregnancy
is not mere luck—it helped that she had a screaming fit on their wedding
night, that she and Grandcourt were in a prolonged icy battle throughout their marriage, and that she did not throw the rope to him as he was
drowning. Like Hetty and Dorothea before her, she makes some conscious decisions that help her to avoid motherhood. All the main characters, then, fulfill, in some form, their wishes and quests concerning
mothers and mothering, albeit not always as they had at first envisioned.

In some ways Eliot's treatment of mothering in this novel is similar
to that in earlier works: many mothers are often absent here as they have
been in previous novels, and we once again see a female protagonist
hoping to avoid pregnancy. But in *Daniel Deronda,* Eliot seems much
more eager to explore in depth mother/child relationships in various forms

and to celebrate them. She does not marginalize mothers or hesitate to show their importance. The dominance of the mother motif in this work makes one wonder why critics have so often suggested that the book lacks unity, that it falls into two stories—Deronda's and Gwendolen's.[33] Both stories are bound together by a longing toward mother and an exploration of mother/child relations and how they motivate adult behavior.

Perhaps in this last novel Eliot turned her focus more toward mother/child relationships because she was coming more to terms with her own mothering impulses. As Pauline Nestor indicates in quoting from Eliot's letters, "she counted 'the growth of a maternal feeling towards both men and women who are much younger' as one of the satisfactions of growing older . . . and felt 'conscious of having an unused stock of motherly tenderness.' "[34] As she grew older and had an increasing number of young followers and children in book form, Eliot became more and more a mother figure, and therefore would have less cause to regret her decision not to become a biological mother. In her earlier novels, Eliot may have subconsciously felt the need to defend her iconoclastic decisions to live with Lewes and to avoid parenthood; she did this by recurrently depicting women who would like to or ought to avoid motherhood but eventually don't and are diminished or killed by it. The sad fates of Milly Barton, Caterina Sarti, Dinah, Hetty, and Dorothea could help a woman who has chosen a vocation instead of children feel good about her decision, for even when the parenting is positive the constraints the women face in their roles seem a loss. By the end of her career, Eliot had no need to defend her choice—her works were her best defense, and they had earned her entrance into a society that initially had rejected her for running off with a married man.

The portraits of mothers are never simplistic in Eliot. Even in *Daniel Deronda,* when her sympathy seems most engaged in mother-figures, she avoids showing either Gwendolen or Mirah becoming mothers. *Daniel Deronda* is one of the few books without a parent/child tableau in the end. We've seen that *Adam Bede's* was brief but telling, and *Middlemarch's* was distant and vague, but still the parent/child tableau was there. *Scenes of Clerical Life* ends with a vague picture of Janet surrounded by her adopted daughter's children. Romola mothers her husband's illegitimate children at the end of the novel that bears her name. It is interesting that Eliot makes one of the most maternal, nurturing characters in her works a man, Silas Marner, who serves as both mother and father to the adopted Eppie. Like Mrs. Davilow he resists frustrating his child and does not punish her, and they stay close and affectionate into her adulthood (somehow managing to avoid Gwendolen's narcissism). That novel ends with an Edenic picture of father and daughter in their garden on her wedding day with Eppie proclaiming, " 'O father, . . . what a pretty home ours is! I think nobody could be happier than we are' " (317). No picture in Eliot of biological parents and children resonates quite so positively. *Felix Holt's* last line informs us that Esther and Felix have a son, but not even the vaguest picture is offered of their family life. *Daniel Deronda* concludes with Gwendolen saying she will survive and with Mordecai dying; none of the major characters yet has any children. It seems Eliot had become more sympathetic, understanding, and celebratory about mothers and mothering by the end of her career, but biological motherhood was still a conclusion with which she was uncomfortable.

Notes

1. Bonnie Zimmerman, " 'The Mother's History' in George Eliot's Life, Literature, and Political Ideology," in *The Lost Tradition: Mothers and Daughters in Literature,* ed. Cathy N. Davidson and E. M. Broner (New York: Frederick Ungar, 1980), 83.

2. Gillian Beer, *George Eliot* (Bloomington: Indiana University Press, 1986), 112.

3. Zimmerman, 82.

4. Pauline Nestor, *Female Friendships and Communities: Charlotte Brontë, George Eliot, Elizabeth Gaskell* (Oxford: Clarendon Press, 1985), 179.

5. Beer, 112.

6. Gordon S. Haight, *George Eliot: A Biography* (New York: Oxford University Press, 1968), 21.

7. Ibid., 535.

8. Ibid., 205; Nestor, 157.

9. Haight, 332; Sandra M. Gilbert and Susan Gubar, *The Madwoman in the Attic: The Woman Writer and the Nineteenth-century Literary Imagination* (New Haven: Yale University Press, 1984), 476; Zimmerman, 85.

10. Haight, 452, 494.

11. Ibid., 519.

12. Ibid., 364.

13. Quoted in Haight, 533.

14. Rosemarie Bodenheimer, *The Real Life of Mary Ann Evans: George Eliot, Her Letters and Fiction* (Ithaca: Cornell University Press, 1994), 259.

15. Beer, 167.

16. *The George Eliot Letters,* Vol. 1, ed. Gordon S. Haight (New Haven: Yale University Press, 1954), 66.

17. Ibid., 72.

18. Quoted in Elaine Showalter, *A Literature of Their Own: British Women Novelists from Brontë to Lessing* (Princeton, NJ: Princeton University Press, 1977), 68.

19. Quoted in Haight, 396.

20. Mason Harris, "Infanticide and Respectability: Hetty Sorrel as Abandoned Child in *Adam Bede*," *The Critical Response to George Eliot*, ed. Karen L. Pangallo (Westport, CT: Greenwood Press, 1994), 54.

21. Ibid., 53.

22. Ibid., 55.

23. Zimmerman, 85; *The George Eliot Letters*, Vol. 3, ed. Gordon S. Haight (New Haven: Yale University Press, 1954-55), 117; *The George Eliot Letters*, Vol. 4, ed. Gordon S. Haight (New York: Yale University Press, 1954-55), 236.

24. Zimmerman, 83.

25. Ibid.

26. Gilbert and Gubar, 486.

27. Zimmerman, 92; Beer, 110-11.

28. Beer, 111.

29. Zimmerman, 92.

30. Ibid.

31. Dorothy Dinnerstein, *The Mermaid and the Minotaur: Sexual Arrangements and Human Malaise* (New York: Harper and Row, 1976), 166, 161, 176, 191.

32. Nancy Chodorow, *The Reproduction of Mothering: Psychoanalysis and the Sociology of Gender* (Berkeley: University of California Press, 1978), 69.

33. See James Caron's "The Rhetoric of Magic in *Daniel Deronda*" in *The Critical Response to George Eliot*, 207. Caron points out that criticism of *Daniel Deronda* falls into two camps: those who feel the novel falls into two stories that do not cohere, and those who feel the two stories are more integrally connected than often supposed.

34. Nestor, 157.

Chapter 7

Conclusion

Mother is the name of God in the lips and hearts of little children. . . .
—William Thackeray, *Vanity Fair*

I hated the thought of having children and have no adoration for very little babies. . . .
—Queen Victoria to her eldest daughter, Victoria, March 16, 1859.[1]

Let each mother then engrave upon the heart of her son such an image of feminine virtue and loveliness, as may make it sufficient for him to turn his eyes inward in order to draw thence a power sufficient to combat evil, and to preserve him from wretchedness.
—Sarah Lewis, *Woman's Mission*[2]

The dominance of mothers, mother-longing, and the fear of mothers and motherhood are factors in mid-Victorian novels that have not been duly appreciated. Whether characters are idolizing, attacking, avoiding, or trying not to become mothers, mothers and motherhood dramatically shape their actions and the themes and structures of major mid-Victorian narratives. The intense onslaught of unrealistic sociocultural pressures from conduct books, periodicals, medical texts, and the image that Queen Victoria projected exacerbated mothers' guilt and frustrations and the frustrations of others toward mothers. The Victorian maternal ideal appealed to the infantile desire for complete, all-encompassing, womblike love and devotion, a desire that few if any ever really grow out of. The longing for that love reverberates in the sad "want of something" that haunted Charles Dickens throughout his life and that led to attacks against mothers in his novels; it manifests itself in

William Thackeray's ideal but incestuous mothers and in the longing of Charlotte Brontë's heroines (and some George Eliot protagonists) for a mystical union reminiscent of the initial harmony between fetus and mother. The fear of becoming a mother under such impossible demands, a fear understood only by the women authors in this study, causes both Brontë and Eliot to depict heroines who flee or at least temporarily avoid motherhood.

In examining major mid-Victorian novels by Dickens, Brontë, Thackeray, and Eliot, it would be foolish not to look at the biographies of the novelists, in addition to the sociohistoric context, since the tensions of the fiction could not help but be influenced by personal psychological dynamics. The relationships that these authors had with their mothers diverged radically from the ideal being promulgated all around them as they were writing. The discrepancy between the ideal and the real heightened the unavoidable frustrations that any child feels toward the mother who fails to meet every need, who encourages the separation from that original, blissful union between mother and child. Dickens demonstrates the greatest bitterness toward mother-figures in his novels; interestingly, he also had his mother around more than any of the other authors on whom I focus. Of the four major authors I examine in this book, Charlotte Brontë had the least exposure to her mother, and in her works I've traced a greater longing for a maternal union than in the novels of any of the other writers. There seems to be a direct correlation in these writers between the amount of time spent with mother and the amount of hostilities vented toward maternal figures in their works. Less is more, it seems, when it comes to Victorian mothering. Psychoanalytic mothering theorists would argue that this pattern is natural, that the increase in hostilities felt by Dickens, for example, is a result of his mother exacerbating the initial frustrations she caused him as an infant by her later behavior when he was a boy and then an adult. Children who do not have their mothers around to continue frustrating them naturally would develop less hostilities, as is the case with Brontë and Eliot (unless the mother died in the first three years of the child's life, in which case other psychological disturbances would be likely). Thackeray's mother was both around and not around—alive, yes, but often at a geographical distance; although she certainly provided him with ample frustrations as an adult, his maternal characterizations seem to be shaped both by the longing for an ideal union with a mother and an awareness of the potential destructiveness of mothers.[3]

These authors compensate for unsatisfactory mothering by becoming the ideal mothers to their own texts. In the time, energy, sacrifice, and suffering they devoted to their creations, these authors met the highest ideals of mothering set forth by Sarah Ellis, Sarah Lewis, and Isabella Beeton. But frustrations and dangers abounded in these artistic-mothering relationships as well. Dickens and Thackeray both worked themselves to early deaths. Eliot felt scourged by her books, and both she and Brontë were paralyzed by negative criticisms of their works.

The mothers in novels by mid-Victorian novelists offer more to explore in terms of extremes, contradictions, and subterranean tensions than those in later Victorian works because the mother ideal is strongest in mid-century and is most powerfully shaping the novelists whether they submit to it, resist it, or both. In the late Victorian age, although the ideal still persisted in the popular ethos, major novelists such as Thomas Hardy and George Gissing gave it less heed, thereby avoiding the strange mixes of angels and monsters in Dickens and Thackeray and the strange mix of yearning toward and avoidance of mothers and motherhood in Brontë and Eliot. The ideal was getting a bit hackneyed. The "new woman" of the 1880s and 1890s became a more compelling figure, with her demands for equality and greater professional options.[4] No new writers of guidebooks for women had emerged to be as prolific and influential as Sarah Ellis had been, and Queen Victoria had moved beyond childbearing age and therefore no longer provided the country with such a famous and pronounced maternal image. The best novelists' tastes for sentiment had been sated, and writers were turning to more realistic, less extreme portrayals that better reflected the uncertainty of the times. The ideal survived in expectations of mothers, particularly middle-class mothers—many aspects of it even linger with us today. But the high tide of social and psychological forces that helped to create the energy, complexity, and rich tensions of mother-figures in great mid-Victorian novels had begun to ebb.

Notes

1. *Dearest Child: Letters Between Queen Victoria and the Princess Royal 1858-61,* ed. Roger Fulford (New York: Holt, Rinehart and Winston, 1964), 167.

2. Sarah Lewis, *Woman's Mission* (Boston: William Crosby & Co. 1840), 33.

3. It is interesting to note that three of the four featured authors in this study lost or were separated from their mothers when they were five

years old: Brontë's mother died when she was five; Eliot and Thackeray were sent away to school at this age. While these early losses certainly caused pain and unfulfilled longing, they also prevented continued frustrations and therefore may explain in part why Brontë, Eliot, and Thackeray demonstrate less hostility in their maternal characterizations than does Dickens.

4. Richard D. Altick, *Victorian People and Ideas* (New York: W. W. Norton, 1973), 59.

Bibliography

Primary Sources

Major Works by Anne Brontë

Agnes Grey. Introduction by Anne Smith. London: Dent, 1985.

Major Works by Charlotte Brontë

Jane Eyre. Ed. Richard J. Dunn. Norton Critical Edition. New York: W. W. Norton, 1971.

The Professor. Ed. Heather Glen. New York: Penguin, 1989.

Shirley. Ed. Andrew and Judith Hook. New York: Penguin, 1987.

Villette. Introduction by Margaret Lane. New York: Dutton, 1978.

Major Works by Emily Brontë

Wuthering Heights. Ed. William M. Sale, Jr. New York: Norton, 1972.

Major Works by Dickens

Barnaby Rudge. New York: Oxford University Press, 1987.

Bleak House. New York: Oxford University Press, 1987.

Christmas Stories. New York: Oxford University Press, 1987.

David Copperfield. New York: Oxford University Press, 1987.

Dombey and Son. New York: Oxford University Press, 1987.

Great Expectations. New York: Oxford University Press, 1987.

Hard Times. New York: Oxford University Press, 1987.

Little Dorrit. New York: Oxford University Press, 1987.

Martin Chuzzlewit. New York: Oxford University Press, 1987.

The Mystery of Edwin Drood. New York: Oxford University Press, 1987.

Nicholas Nickleby. New York: Oxford University Press, 1987.

The Old Curiosity Shop. New York: Oxford University Press, 1987.

Oliver Twist. New York: Oxford University Press, 1987.

Our Mutual Friend. New York: Oxford University Press, 1987.

The Pickwick Papers. New York: Oxford University Press, 1987.

Sketches by Boz. New York: Oxford University Press, 1987.

A Tale of Two Cities. New York: Oxford University Press, 1987.

The Uncommercial Traveller and Reprinted Pieces. New York: Oxford University Press, 1987.

Major Works by George Eliot

Adam Bede. Edited with introduction by Stephen Gill. New York: Penguin, 1985.

Daniel Deronda. Edited with introduction by Barbara Hardy. New York: Penguin, 1986.

Felix Holt, the Radical. Ed. Fred C. Thomson. Oxford: Clarendon Press, 1980.

Middlemarch. Ed. Rosemary Ashton. New York: Penguin, 1994.

Romola. Ed. Andrew Sanders. New York: Penguin, 1980.

Scenes of Clerical Life. Edited with introduction by Thomas A. Noble. New York: Oxford University Press, 1988.

Silas Marner. New York: Lancer Books, 1968.

Major Works by Thackeray

The History of Henry Esmond. Ed. John Sutherland and Michael Greenfield with an introduction by John Sutherland. New York: Penguin, 1987.

The History of Pendennis: His Fortunes and Misfortunes, His Friends and His Greatest Enemy. Edited with an introduction by George Saintsbury. New York: Oxford University Press, 1952.

Lovel the Widower. Boston: Estes and Lauriat, 1881.

Vanity Fair. New York: Penguin, 1985.

The Virginians; A Tale of the Last Century. Ed. George Saintsbury. New York: Oxford University Press, n.d.

Secondary Sources

Ackroyd, Peter. *Dickens*. New York: HarperPerennial, 1992.

Adams, Maurianne. "*Jane Eyre*: Woman's Estate." In *Critical Essays on Charlotte Brontë*, ed. Barbara Timm Gates. Boston: G. K. Hall, 1990, 181-199.

Al-Hibri, Azizah. "Reproduction, Mothering, and the Origins of Patriarchy." In *Mothering: Essays in Feminist Theory*, ed. Joyce Trebilcot. Totowa, NJ: Rowman & Allanheld, 1983, 84-88.

Altick, Richard D. *Victorian People and Ideas*. New York: W. W. Norton, 1973.

Balbus, Isaac D. "Disciplining Women: Michel Foucault and the Power of Feminist Discourse." In *After Foucault: Humanistic Knowledge, Postmodern Challenges*. New Brunswick, NJ: Rutgers University Press, 1988, 138-60.

Barickman, Richard, Susan MacDonald, and Myra Stark. *Corrupt Relations: Dickens, Thackeray, Trollope, Collins, and the Victorian Sexual System*. New York: Columbia University Press, 1982.

Beer, Gillian. *George Eliot*. Bloomington: Indiana University Press, 1986.

Beeton, Isabella. *Mrs. Beeton's Household Management*. Rev. ed. London: Ward, Lock & Co., 1949.

Bodenheimer, Rosemarie. *The Real Life of Mary Ann Evans: George Eliot, Her Letters and Fiction*. Ithaca: Cornell University Press, 1994.

Bowlby, John. "Changing Theories of Childhood Since Freud." In *Freud in Exile: Psychoanalysis and its Vicissitudes*, ed. Edward Timms and Naomi Segal. New Haven, CT: Yale University Press, 1988, 230-40.

Branca, Patricia. *Silent Sisterhood: Middle Class Women in the Victorian Home*. Pittsburgh: Carnegie-Mellon University Press, 1975.

Bull, Thomas. *Hints to Mothers, for the Management of Health During the Period of Pregnancy, and in the Lying-in-Room; with an Exposure of Popular Errors in Connexion with those Subjects*. 3rd ed. New York: Wiley and Putnam, 1842.

Carey, John. *Thackeray: Prodigal Genius*. Boston: Faber and Faber, 1977.

———. *The Violent Effigy: A Study of Dickens' Imagination*. Boston: Faber, 1973.

Caron, James. "The Rhetoric of Magic in *Daniel Deronda*." In *The Critical Response to George Eliot*, ed. Karen L. Pangallo. Westport, CT: Greenwood Press, 1994, 207-14.

Chodorow, Nancy. *The Reproduction of Mothering: Psychoanalysis and the Sociology of Gender*. Berkeley: University of California Press, 1978.

Currie, Richard A. "Surviving Maternal Loss: Transitional Relatedness in Dickens's Esther Summerson." *Dickens Quarterly* 6.2 (1989): 60-66.

Dearest Child: Letters Between Queen Victoria and the Princess Royal 1858-61. Ed. Roger Fulford. New York: Holt, Rinehart and Winston, 1964.

Dinnerstein, Dorothy. *The Mermaid and the Minotaur: Sexual Arrangements and Human Malaise.* New York: Harper and Row, 1976.

Eldredge, Patricia. "The Lost Self of Esther Summerson: A Horneyan Interpretation of *Bleak House.*" In *Third Force Psychology and the Study of Literature,* ed. Bernard J. Paris. Toronto: Associated University Presses, 1986, 136-55.

Ellis, Sarah. *First Impressions; Or, Hints to Those Who Would Make Home Happy.* New York: Appleton, 1849.

——. *The Mothers of England: Their Influence and Responsibility.* New York: D. Appleton & Co., 1844.

——. *The Wives of England: Their Relative Duties, Domestic Influence and Social Obligations.* New York: J. & H. G. Langley, 1843.

——. *The Women of England: Their Social Duties and Domestic Habits.* New York: J. & H. G. Langley, 1843.

Fine, Reuben. *The History of Psychoanalysis.* New expanded ed. New York: Continuum, 1990.

First, Elsa. "Mothering, Hate and Winnicott." In *Representations of Motherhood,* ed. Donna Bassin, Margaret Honey, and Meryle Mahrer Kaplan. New Haven: Yale University Press, 1994, 147-61.

Gaskell, Elizabeth. *The Life of Charlotte Brontë.* Ed. Alan Shelston. New York: Penguin, 1985.

Gates, Barbara Timm, ed. *Critical Essays on Charlotte Brontë.* Boston: G. K. Hall, 1990.

The George Eliot Letters. Ed. Gordon S. Haight. New Haven: Yale University Press, 1954.

Gilbert, Sandra M. "A Dialogue of Self and Soul: Plain Jane's Progress." In *Critical Essays on Charlotte Brontë,* ed. Barbara Timm Gates. Boston: G. K. Hall, 1990, 156-80.

Gilbert, Sandra M. and Susan Gubar. *The Madwoman in the Attic: The Woman Writer and the Nineteenth-Century Literary Imagination.* New Haven: Yale University Press, 1984.

Gubar, Susan. "The Genesis of Hunger, According to *Shirley.*" In *Critical Essays on Charlotte Brontë,* ed. Barbara Timm Gates. Boston: G. K. Hall, 1990, 232-51.

Gilligan, Carol. *In A Different Voice: Psychological Theory and Women's Development*. Cambridge, MA: Harvard University Press, 1982.

Goodman, Marci Renee. "'I'll Follow the Other': Tracing the (M)other in *Bleak House*." *Dickens Studies Annual* 19 (1990): 147-67.

Haight, Gordon S. *George Eliot: A Biography*. New York: Oxford University Press, 1968.

Halliday, Andrew. "Mothers." *All the Year Round* Sept. 9, 1865: 157-59.

Harris, Mason. "Infanticide and Respectability: Hetty Sorrel as Abandoned Child in *Adam Bede*." In *The Critical Response to George Eliot*, ed. Karen L. Pangallo. Westport, CT: Greenwood Press, 1994, 49-67.

Holbrook, David. *Charles Dickens and the Image of Woman*. New York: New York University Press, 1993.

Homans, Margaret. "Victoria's Sovereign Obedience: Portraits of the Queen as Wife and Mother." In *Victorian Literature and the Victorian Visual Imagination*, eds. Carol T. Christ and John O. Jordan. Berkeley: University of California Press, 1995, 169-97.

Hunt, Leigh. "Childbed: A Prose Poem." *Monthly Repository* New enlarged series, 1 (1837): 356.

Ingham, Patricia. *Dickens, Women and Language*. Toronto: University of Toronto Press, 1992.

Johnson, Edgar. *Charles Dickens: His Tragedy and Triumph*. 2 vols. New York: Simon and Schuster, 1952.

Kaplan, Fred. *Dickens: A Biography*. New York: William Morrow, 1988.

Klein, Melanie. *Love, Guilt, and Reparation and Other Works 1921-1945*. Introduction by R. E. Money-Kyrle. New York: The Free Press (Macmillan), 1975.

The Letters of Charles Dickens. Pilgrim Edition, vol. 1. Ed. Madeline House et al. Oxford: Clarendon Press, 1965.

The Letters of Charles Dickens. Pilgrim Edition, vol. 2. Ed. Madeline House et al. Oxford: Clarendon Press, 1969.

The Letters of Charles Dickens. Pilgrim Edition, vol. 4. Ed. Kathleen Tillotson. Oxford: Clarendon Press, 1977.

The Letters of Charles Dickens. Pilgrim Edition, vol. 5. Ed. Graham Storey and K. J. Fielding. Oxford: Clarendon Press, 1981.

The Letters of Charles Dickens. Pilgrim Edition, vol. 6. Ed. Graham Storey, Kathleen Tillotson, and Nina Burgis. Oxford: Clarendon Press, 1988.

The Letters and Private Papers of William Makepeace Thackeray. Collected and edited by Gordon N. Ray. New York: Farrar, Strauss and Giroux, 1980.

Lewis, Sarah. *Woman's Mission.* Boston: William Crosby and Co., 1840.

Lynn, Eliza. "A Mother." *Household Words* April 4, 1857: 332-36.

McKnight, Natalie. *Idiots, Madmen and Other Prisoners in Dickens.* New York: St. Martin's Press, 1993.

McMaster, Juliet. *Thackeray: The Major Novels.* Manchester, England: University of Toronto Press, 1971.

Nestor, Pauline. *Female Friendships and Communities: Charlotte Brontë, George Eliot, Elizabeth Gaskell.* Oxford: Clarendon Press, 1985.

The Nonesuch Letters of Charles Dickens. Ed. Walter Dexter. Vol. 3, 1858-1870. Bloomsbury: The Nonesuch Press, 1938.

Paglia, Camille. *Sexual Personae: Art and Decadence from Nefertiti to Emily Dickinson.* New York: Vintage, 1991.

Peters, Margot. *Unquiet Soul: A Biography of Charlotte Brontë.* New York: Doubleday, 1975.

Phoenix, Ann, and Anne Woollett. "Motherhood: Social Construction, Politics and Psychology." In *Motherhood: Meanings, Practices and Ideologies.* Ed. Ann Phoenix, Anne Woolett, and Eva Lloyd. London: Sage, 1991, 13-27.

Ray, Gordon. *The Buried Life: A Study of the Relation Between Thackeray's Fiction and His Personal History.* London: Oxford University Press, 1952.

———. *Thackeray: The Uses of Adversity (1811-1846).* New York: McGraw-Hill, 1955.

Rich, Adrienne. *Of Woman Born: Motherhood as Experience and Institution.* New York: W. W. Norton, 1986.

———. "Jane Eyre: The Temptations of a Motherless Woman." In *Critical Essays on Charlotte Brontë.* Ed. Barbara Timm Gates. Boston: G. K. Hall, 1990, 142-55.

St. Aubyn, Giles. *Queen Victoria.* New York: Atheneum, 1992.

Sawicki, Jana. *Disciplining Foucault: Feminism, Power and the Body.* New York: Routledge, 1991.

Segal, Naomi. "Freud and the Question of Women." In *Freud in Exile: Psychoanalysis and Its Vicissitudes.* Ed. Edward Timms and Naomi Segal. New Haven: Yale University Press, 1988, 241-53.

Selected Letters of Charles Dickens. Edited and arranged by David Paroissien. Boston: Twayne, 1985.

Shapiro, Arnold. "Public Themes and Private Lives: Social Criticism in *Shirley*." In *Critical Essays on Charlotte Brontë*. Ed. Barbara Timm Gates. Boston: G. K. Hall, 1990, 223-32.

Shires, Linda. "Of Maenads, Mothers and Feminized Males: Victorian Readings of the French Revolution." In *Rewriting the Victorians: Theory, History and the Politics of Gender.* Ed. Linda Shires. New York: Routledge, 1992, 147-65.

Showalter, Elaine. *A Literature of Their Own: British Women Novelists from Brontë to Lessing*. Princeton, NJ: Princeton University Press, 1977.

Shuttleworth, Sally. "Demonic Mothers: Ideologies of Bourgeois Motherhood in the Mid-Victorian Era." In *Rewriting the Victorians: Theory, History, and the Politics of Gender.* Ed. Linda M. Shires. New York: Routledge, 1992.

Slater, Michael. *Dickens and Women*. Stanford: Stanford University Press, 1983.

Smart, Carol. "Disruptive Bodies and Unruly Sex: The Regulation of Reproduction and Sexuality in the Nineteenth Century." In *Regulating Womanhood; Historical Essays on Marriage, Motherhood and Sexuality.* New York: Routledge, 1992, 7-32.

Storey, Gladys. *Dickens and Daughters*. New York: Haskell House, 1971.

Tayler, Irene. *Holy Ghosts: The Male Muses of Emily and Charlotte Brontë*. New York: Columbia University Press, 1990.

Thurer, Shari L. *The Myths of Motherhood: How Culture Reinvents the Good Mother.* Boston: Houghton Mifflin, 1994.

Tillotson, Geoffrey and Donald Hawes, eds. *Thackeray: The Critical Heritage.* London: Routledge & Kegan Paul, 1968.

Ward, John C. "The Virtues of the Mothers: Powerful Women in *Bleak House*." *Dickens Studies Newsletter* 14.2 (1983): 37-42.

Watkins, Gwen. *Dickens in Search of Himself: Recurrent Themes and Characters in the Work of Charles Dickens*. Totowa, NJ: Barnes & Noble, 1987.

Zimmerman, Bonnie. "'The Mother's History' in George Eliot's Life, Literature, and Political Ideology." In *The Lost Tradition: Mothers and Daughters in Literature.* Ed. Cathy N. Davidson and E. M. Broner. New York: Frederick Ungar, 1980, 81-94.

Index